On Your Mark
Kriss Akabusi

On Your Mark

Kriss Akabusi

The Bible Reading Fellowship
OPENING THE BIBLE

Published by
The Bible Reading Fellowship
Peter's Way, Sandy Lane West
Oxford OX4 5HG
ISBN 0 7459 3515 X
Albatross Books Pty Ltd
PO Box 320, Sutherland
NSW 2232, Australia
ISBN 0 7324 1544 6

First edition 1996
10 9 8 7 6 5 4 3 2 1 0

Acknowledgments
Unless otherwise stated, scripture is
taken from The Holy Bible, New
International Version, copyright © 1973,
1978, 1984 by International Bible
Society. Used by permission of Hodder
and Stoughton Limited.

A catalogue record for this book is
available from the British Library

Printed and bound in Great Britain
by Cox and Wyman Limited, Reading

Contents

Preface

When I first met Kriss Akabusi he had a thirst quenched only by an ocean of answers and a hunger satisfied with a diet of critical texts alone. Many of my classes were interrupted by this transplanted Brit. standing in the lecture hall engaged in passionate inquiry. Arms flailing, pen and notes in opposing hands, his books on neighbours' laps, his melange of thoughts naive yet riveting. His simple questions were those found in conversations among classical scholars whose names were unknown to him. I watched him elude crowds to read St Paul, Ambrose and Augustine. He kept in the corners to devour Abelard, Kant and Bonhoeffer. He toted Nietzsche, Hegel and Rousseau from the library. He parked in the far reaches of the lot to catch precious minutes with Thoreau, Hawthorn and Tolstoy.

He wanted to learn, at first for learning's sake—then to prepare for leadership. He came to understand that abstract teachings have produced concrete results, both good and bad, reforming and razing the fabrics of societies. He found that leaders are made for various reasons: competency often but not always a criteria. Paramount decisions are made and followed by design or by default. Leaders perceptive, concerned, and situated to make decisions do so by design. Others accept or endorse decisions be default.

Kriss also learned the process of deciding right from wrong, and he came to the logical conclusion that education is not about gathering information and saying that we can all be right. Conversely, some decisions are better than others, regardless of the source, individual or corporate. He learned the art of critical thinking. Re-evaluating his initial beliefs, weighing those tenets against the multi-faceted data, and then refining, sometimes changing his foundational maxims. His religious beliefs became all the more present, yet with seasoned and articulate speech.

Kriss managed perfect grades amidst all the pressures and distractions of Olympic training and success. He knew that his legs would soon lose their youth. My God-given question for Kriss was and is one of *opus*, 'Will your greatest contribution to society by your medals, or have these positioned you for some greater work?'

His eyes were often on the beloved country he ran for and now strives to serve. America could benefit from such an individual, and I am sure that England recognizes well its own. He is a sterling example of courage and sacrifice, the manifestation of all that is good in the educational and religious traditions so often castigated. The Queen should be applauded for recognizing his contributions and endorsing him to facilitate the young odysseys of children.

Of course, Kriss Akabusi is fun. Exhausting and exhilarating. And please be assured, those Akabusi smiles run deep into his soul—not fronts for a mask but exclamation marks for his beliefs.

He has become a friend—not just because we mutually enjoy personalities, but also the first principles behind our persons. Several times since his last return to England he has called me from his car phone, usually en route to the BBC and stuck in the traffic. Seconds after initial greetings we are headlong in discussion about his current reading. He has read through the lists of books passed his way and is always interested in more. Now he sends lists my way.

Imagine receiving an enthusiastic call from a lively Brit, stuck in London traffic before his breakfast hour, and his first sentences are: 'D-o-c-t-o-r Pass-or-Fail! Greetings my friend! Great to talk with you. Now what do you think about Book Seven of Plato's *Republic*?'

Dr Jerry Pattengale, Administrative Director, The Scriptorium: Center For Christian Antiquities Grand Haven, Michigan

Foreword

One Sunday in 1987, the tall figure of Kriss Akabusi walked into our church. To us he was a nobody, just another visitor to the morning service. Granted, he looked fitter than most and his broad smile made this man very endearing. Little did I realize that that day was to be the beginning of a warm and close friendship with a man who later would become a world-class athlete and a household name. Somehow Kriss has taken all this in his stride, and fame has not changed him. In many ways he has used the opportunities that have come his way in life to become a better Christian.

As his pastor, I have spent many hours with Kriss and have seen a deep love for God's word become a very important focus in his life. His sharp mind has pressed him to search the scriptures and discover the truth of the Bible. I began to see in Kriss the seeds of a good biblical apologist as he started his studies in St Mark's Gospel. Over some two years he took our church through this book and presented the life and ministry of Christ in a fresh and exciting way. It soon became clear to me that these studies were noteworthy enough to be put in book form, and I am delighted that this has come about.

Kriss in his own inimitable style portrays the Gospel of Mark in a way that you will find both refreshing and challenging. You will be refreshed as you consider the life of Christ. You will be challenged to consider your life in the light of all that Jesus said and did.

We're not all called to be famous or world champions—but we are called to follow Christ. If this book encourages you to do that, then Kriss will have reached his goal. As Kriss says: 'Only when I met Jesus did I grasp the meaning of life and find true meaning and satisfaction.'

Paul R. Finn, Pastor, Southampton Christian Fellowship

Introduction

This book has its origins in the lecture rooms of Azusa Pacific University in the USA. I spent what amounted to two years studying various courses ranging from philosophy through to history and biblical studies. On my return to the UK, I developed a series of sermons which I preached to my home church, the Southampton Christian Fellowship, over a period of two years. I am grateful to Pastor Paul Finn and the elders of the church for giving me the opportunity to undertake the series.

Among the many positive acclaims I received for my previous book, *Kriss Akabusi On Track with the Bible*, there was one negative comment that continued to persist: 'Why do we ask people to write a Christian book just because they are famous in other areas of life?' My answer is simple. I am a Christian with firmly held views and beliefs. I am often called to give an account of those views by the public—be it from business, universities, schools or the sports field—for the faith that I have within me. It is my belief that God calls different people at different times to prominence, to shine the spotlight on them for just that reason. I believe that this is my ministry.

This book makes no claim to be the last word on Mark. It represents purely my thoughts on Mark at this moment in time. This is my experience of reading Mark's Gospel and of trying to live out the message of the book in my own life. This is a subjective account. These are things which have affected me and challenged me as I have tried to live out the message of this Gospel. I certainly make no claim that this is the only way to interpret Mark.

At this juncture I would like to thank Stuart Weir of Christians in Sport who has turned the sermons into a book. Can you imagine that poor man? He had to drive around the country listening to my sermons on tape!

I became a Christian in 1987, and an important step on the road to faith was finding a Bible in my room at the Commonwealth Games in Edinburgh in 1986. I read the New Testament right through in two weeks. I still try to read the Bible every day because it is my way of understanding what God has to say about me as an individual and about the world as a whole. It is my way of understanding what God has to say about himself.

It is my hope and prayer that, as you read this book, you will find my comments helpful, and it will stimulate you to ask further questions. What really matters, however, is not what I think, but what God has revealed. God said to the prophet Isaiah: 'my word that goes out from my mouth: It will not return to me empty, but will accomplish what I desire and achieve the purpose for which I sent it' (Isaiah 55:11—12). May you let God's word speak into your life.

Mark 1

The beginning: The kingdom of God and how Jesus fulfils it

*T*he beginning of the gospel about Jesus Christ, the Son of God. It is written in Isaiah the prophet: 'I will send my messenger ahead of you, who will prepare your way'—'a voice of one calling in the desert, "Prepare the way for the Lord, make straight paths for him."'...

At that time Jesus came from Nazareth in Galilee and was baptised by John in the Jordan.

As Jesus was coming up out of the water, he saw heaven being torn open and the Spirit descending on him like a dove. And a voice came from heaven: 'You are my Son, whom I love; with you I am well pleased.'

Mark 1:1–3, 9–11

My Olympic bronze medal symbolizes the peak of my achievement—I worked very hard over ten years, over the 1992 season and particularly during the month leading up to the Olympics to gain that medal. I had a target, and I hit it.

Because I really wanted to win an Olympic medal in the 400 metres hurdles, I was very purposeful about working hard towards that goal. In fact, athletically I did everything perfectly to the exclusion of everything else to gain that victory. I didn't take any extra weight—I couldn't have run in my street clothes—I wouldn't have made it. I couldn't take any extra baggage.

On your way towards a victory like that you become a very popular figure in the media, but I couldn't stop and spend time with the media people—I couldn't take time to wine and dine—I had to be very single-minded on my way towards that medal, that victory.

In fact over those ten years, and especially in the last year, there was a definite plan, a clear awareness of the steps I had to take and progress checks I had to make in order to ensure that I achieved that victory.

In a way, it's exactly the same with my life as I walk with the Lord—there is a spiritual victory to be won. Paul in his letter to the church at Philippi refers to this as 'God's call through Christ Jesus to the life above'. Christ has already won the supreme victory and opened up the way to heaven for us, but we still have to make our way towards that victory.

Paul talks about achieving this victory in terms running a race, disregarding everything else that is around you to get to your goal. Even on the day of an Olympic final itself you are so close to your dream and yet you are still far away. No matter how close I came, if I did not win I would not have got that prize. I would not have got that medal. And so it can be with us in our lives. We can be so close to Christ, so close to the victory, so close to that prize—we can even see it. And yet the troubles in life, the things that come along and the sufferings can distract you from that straight line, from the path. After all that disciplined preparation, and ten years of training, you're almost there, but you can be deflected. The important thing is to be focused, to be single-minded.

Mark gives us a snapshot of Christ on his way to victory.

Christ had many distractions and could easily have missed the mark (if that is possible with God) if he hadn't set his eyes on Jerusalem, on his purpose, on the victory. There was the distraction of opposition, of temptation, the struggle in Gethsemane. There was the adulation of the crowds who wanted to make him king. There were those who wanted to push him in a different direction: to become a Messiah who would throw the Romans out of Palestine. However Jesus was not to be deflected. As Luke puts it, 'Jesus resolutely set out for Jerusalem.'

When Jesus was crucified in Jerusalem, it initially looked like defeat—but it was really the greatest victory in human history. When he rose again we actually saw the victory, as he stood there with his 'gold medal', if I can be so crude. The resurrection was the ultimate victory. And hopefully we will see that purpose, that single-mindedness. We will see the taking off of everything else to run that race, to be lean, to be in shape, to gain that prize.

Mark's first words are: 'The beginning of the gospel'. Luke and Matthew's Gospels give us the genealogies and the story of Jesus' birth, which are very important, but that is not where Mark begins 'the gospel'. Gospel means 'good news', so what Mark is actually saying is 'now for the good news'. This is the beginning of the good news. We need good news because we are fallen people and, as far as we are concerned, that is bad news.

When I became a Christian people used to say, 'Christians are the people who need a crutch in their life. Christians are the people who are weak, who need something.' I've got news for you. They're right!

Christians are the people who need a crutch, who are the weak people, those who realize they need help. Who realize that they haven't got the answers, that they are sick. The world is sick, the world is fighting against itself; people don't love each other. They don't realize that the reason they don't love each other is because of this illness in them. Christians are the people who really understand that bad news is staring them in the face, that they are spiritually terminally ill and they need the good news. That good news is Jesus.

This is the statement that Mark is making. He is saying that he is going to tell us about Jesus, the Saviour, about his purpose, about how he walked on towards that prize, how he was steadfast and single-minded. The Gospel of Mark is a call to the individual to consider the claims of Christ: Son of God and Son of man. It is his plan and purpose to reconcile sinful man to holy God.

Just then a man in their synagogue who was possessed by an evil spirit cried out, 'What do you want with us, Jesus of Nazareth? Have you come to destroy us? I know who you are—the Holy One of God!' 'Be quiet!' said Jesus sternly. 'Come out of him!' The evil spirit shook the man violently and came out of him with a shriek. The people were all so amazed that they asked each other, 'What is this? A new teaching—and with authority! He even gives orders to evil spirits and they obey him.'

Mark 1:23–27

Nobody likes a loud mouth, one who tells everyone who he is and what he is capable of. Action speaks louder than words. We like to see people accomplish things rather than talk about them. Imagine if I talked a good race but never performed one. What would you think? The world is full of talkers, not doers. In athletics I meet many people who say, 'Next season, I'm going to do this or that'—well, I'm still waiting. I don't know what the demon's motives were for proclaiming Jesus' ministry or deity but Jesus was not going to be rushed into talking about it or forcing it to happen now. His victory at Calvary would be adequate proclamation of his purpose and deity.

Very early in the morning, while it was still dark, Jesus got up, left the house and went off to a solitary place, where he prayed. Simon and his companions went to look for him, and when they found him, they exclaimed: 'Everyone is looking for you!' Jesus replied, 'Let us go somewhere else—to the nearby villages—so that I can preach there also. That is why I have come.' So he travelled throughout Galilee, preaching in their synagogues and driving out demons.

Mark 1:35–39

Jesus has come to proclaim the gospel. He performs miracles and he has shown his authority, his fame is spreading. So there's a big popular following of Jesus. But that doesn't mean that the popular following is a righteous following. This popularity was because suddenly this man had come in here, teaching and doing miracles. The people were looking for excitement and sensation. 'Hey, what's he doing?' And Jesus is saying, 'Look I don't need that sort of PR job, all right? I've got a purpose and my purpose isn't to have this PR machine and all these people coming around and clouding the issue.'

The point is that when you become popular people want your time and they detract from your job. When I was an athlete preparing for the Olympics, I used to get invitations to do all sorts of things—to see the mayor, to come to this dinner and all of this could have distracted me from my real purpose.

As an athlete, I had to be focused, to be tunnel-visioned. I was focused on the Olympics and getting to that final in peak condition to do the business. I had to get my priorities right. I had to put in the work, do the training, eat the right things, get enough rest. There was the temptation to let other things deflect me. Many days it would have been easier to go and take tea with the mayor, but I had to get down to the track and work. 'Just one more time, Kriss. Let's do that one more time.' Each day I had to reaffirm my commitment to the discipline of my training.

Jesus had been in the synagogue and the people were surprised at the authority of his teaching. He cast a demon out of a man in the synagogue and news of him spread throughout the region. We read that the whole town gathered to hear him. Even the demons started proclaiming who Jesus was. Jesus was making an impact in the region. He was recognized wherever he went. The people couldn't get enough of it. This was the business.

But where do we next see Jesus? In a solitary place. In the morning, having risen a long while before daylight, Jesus goes to a solitary place and prays. So Christ is doing all these things but he still has time to pray—he has to get up very early to pray. He can't do it in the daytime, in the car. If he really wants to concentrate and meet with God he goes to a solitary place to pray. He's got a long ordeal ahead and he wants to keep focused on that purpose.

It would have been so easy for Jesus to have stayed there while he was being appreciated. It would have been so easy to have stayed where it was comfortable, to have thought, 'I can't leave now, I'll pray tomorrow.' But no. He was focused. He resolutely set out on his mission. He recognized the importance of prayer and he made the commitment to put the time in when it mattered.

Jesus Christ came with an authority which exceeded that of the scribes and Pharisees

A few days later, when Jesus again entered Capernaum, the people heard that he had come home. So many gathered that there was no room left, not even outside the door, and he preached the word to them. Some men came, bringing to him a paralytic, carried by four of them.

Since they could not get him to Jesus because of the crowd, they made an opening in the roof above Jesus and, after digging through it, lowered the mat the paralysed man was lying on. When Jesus saw their faith, he said to the paralytic, 'Son, your sins are forgiven.'

Now some teachers of the law were sitting there, thinking to themselves, 'Why does this fellow talk like that? He's blaspheming! Who can forgive sins but God alone?' Immediately Jesus knew in his spirit that this was what they were thinking in their hearts, and he said to them, 'Why are you thinking these things? Which is easier: to say to the paralytic, "Your sins are forgiven," or to say, "Get up, take your mat and walk"? But that *you may know that the Son of Man has authority on earth to forgive sins...' He said to the paralytic, 'I tell you, get up, take your mat and go home.'*

He got up, took his mat and walked out in full view of them all. This amazed everyone and they praised God, saying, 'We have never seen anything like this!'

Mark 2:1–12

Jesus entered Capernaum and people heard that he was there. Immediately so many gathered that there was no longer room to receive them, not even near the door, and he preached to them. There were so many people around, not interested in his words, just interested in the sensation. A paralytic came to him, carried by four men (verse 3). When they could not come near him because of the crowd they uncovered the roof where he was. The roofs there were flat and people dried out their vines there and met there to eat together. So you can imagine these guys—they climbed up and could hear where Jesus was. They started undoing the roof. When they had broken through they let down the bed. When Jesus saw their faith he said to the paralytic, 'Son, your sins are forgiven.' That's all he said. Can you imagine that?

This guy's mates had taken a long time getting him down to Jesus. Then Jesus says, 'Son, your sins are forgiven'—that's all. They had not come to listen to a sermon. They wanted action not words, healing action. But those words were powerful and they indicated by what means, power and authority Jesus could heal the sick. The words were as much for the scholars in the crowd as for the sick man.

All the intellectuals there couldn't understand how he could claim to be able to forgive sins unless he was God. The scribes sitting there said, 'Why does this fellow talk like that? He's blaspheming! Who can forgive sins but God alone?' And immediately Jesus said to them 'Why are you thinking these things? Which is easier: to say to the paralytic, "Your sins are forgiven," or to say, "Get up, take your mat and walk"?'

A lot of us say things we don't really mean, but not Jesus. But for Christ it was easier for him to say 'take up your bed and walk'. So he said the hard thing because he had a purpose and that was to go towards Jerusalem and to go on the cross. And you'll find that later on he dies for being the Son of God. It would have been easier for Jesus Christ not to reveal so early in his ministry that he was the Son of God. It would have been much easier for Jesus to say stand up, take up your bed and walk. All the man wanted was physical healing. All Jesus needed to do was restore the man—whom he had created—to full working order. But Jesus wanted the people to realize who he was and what he could do.

Usually, for a man to say 'your sins are forgiven' is not difficult because it requires no tangible evidence. For Jesus, however, the price of saying 'your sins are forgiven' had to be paid on a cross.

Look at verse 10: 'that you may know that the Son of Man has power on earth to forgive sins, he said to the paralytic...'. So because of their unbelief and because he was God he make it clear that he was risking something here. He told this guy, your sins are forgiven—claiming something that only God can claim. To prove he had that authority, he said, 'get up, take your mat and go home'. The man rose up and went out and they were amazed.

As well as showing that Jesus was the Son of God, another purpose of the healing was to glorify God. In all of his miracles the main purpose Christ had in mind was to glorify God, and then to preach the gospel. (We find a third purpose in Mark 8, but more of that later.)

When I was an athlete my purpose was self-evident in

my lifestyle. No words could speak as loud as my daily routine.

What is your purpose in life? Is it to be first, to look after yourself, is your purpose to keep your job? Is your purpose to do all the temporal things that we all do? Or is your purpose to fix your eyes on Jesus to keep on towards the goal, to win 'the prize for which God has called you heavenwards in Christ Jesus' (Philippians 3:14)?

Before I became a Christian, I had a very materialistic view of life. I felt that the purpose of life was to see who could die with the most toys. I was successful. I got a Mercedes, a big house—nice things, but I found that these did not satisfy me. I was looking for more. Only when I met Jesus did I grasp the meaning of life and find true meaning and satisfaction in life.

Do you remember the day you became a Christian, the day you first recognized it, the joy you had? Do you busy yourself with the world around you now, or do you seek Christ? The Psalmist says, 'As the deer pants for streams of water, so my soul pants for you, O God' (Psalm 42:1). Do we enjoy serving Christ and, if necessary, are we ready to suffer for him? What is your purpose: is it self-centred or are you seeking to follow Jesus?

Religion or relationship?

One Sabbath Jesus was going through the cornfields, and as his disciples walked along, they began to pick some ears of corn. The Pharisees said to him, 'Look, why are they doing what is unlawful on the Sabbath?' He answered, 'Have you never read what David did when he and his companions were hungry and in need? In the days of Abiathar the high priest, he entered the house of God and ate the consecrated bread, which is lawful only for priests to eat. And he also gave some to his companions.' Then he said to them, 'The Sabbath was made for man, not man for the Sabbath. So the Son of Man is Lord even of the Sabbath.'

Another time he went into the synagogue, and a man with a shrivelled hand was there. Some of them were looking for a reason to accuse Jesus, so they watched him closely to see if he would heal him on the Sabbath. Jesus said to the man with the shrivelled hand, 'Stand up in front of everyone.' Then Jesus asked them, 'Which is lawful on the Sabbath: to do good or to do evil, to save life or to kill?' But they remained silent. He looked round at them in anger and, deeply distressed at their stubborn hearts, said to the man, 'Stretch out your *hand.' He stretched it out, and his hand was completely restored. Then the Pharisees went out and began to plot with the Herodians how they might kill Jesus.*

Mark 2:23—3:6

Jesus' popularity begins to take off from a small province in Galilee to the whole world but some are against him. The issue could be summarized: religion or relationship?

Religion puts law before need. Relationship puts need before law. The law of Moses said you shall not work on the sabbath. Not content with that, the Pharisees further defined the law to list thirty-nine categories of work which were forbidden.

The people were hungry and they were serving God. The point that God wants to make here is that human need comes before law. The Pharisees had put law before need.

It is very easy to dismiss the Pharisees as a group of people who were off the pace. But perhaps within each of us there is a pharisaical element. Being an athlete and being a military man I like to have things 'bang, bang, bang' in order. I get annoyed if my wife parks her car on the left in the garage because I always park mine on the left! When things contravene our religious framework, we will say: 'No that's not in my law.' We will not cross the road to help someone because it is not in our law.

Jesus says—and shows—that meeting someone's need is more important. Look at verse 2:27. Jesus is saying, in effect: 'Do you really think that, when God created the heavens in six days, he was exhausted and had to rest? No—the reason he rested on the sabbath was for us. Because we will be exhausted if we do not have a day of rest. The sabbath was made because of your need to rest.' Jesus was saying to the Pharisees, 'You have missed the point.'

Dedication to Christ does not mean dedication to ritual.

That is just keeping a form of religion but denying the power to change life. I never had a problem with running on Sunday because I had a relationship with the Lord of the sabbath. I believe that he wanted me to maintain that relationship and do my job for his glory, rather than just keeping the rules about Sunday like a Pharisee.

Religion is death over life. The man with the shrivelled hand had a serious problem. He couldn't work. He needed help but he wasn't going to get it from the Pharisees. Jesus wants me to be thinking about others not just about myself.

Some people were coming to the synagogue, not to glorify God, but to accuse Jesus. They were coming to the synagogue, not to meet each other's needs, but to accuse Jesus. Sometimes I come to church thinking, 'God, you've let me down. You haven't done this. You haven't done that. I expected you to do this. I expected you to do that.' I am thinking about me, me, me. Selfo, besto—who cares about the resto? Jesus says there are people here with needs.

Jesus can see straight away what is happening so he says to the man, 'Stand up.' Jesus wanted to do it in public so that everyone could see what was going to happen. Faith is personal, but not private. Can you imagine being a private athlete? I can break the world record—but only when no one is watching!

The Jews are sitting there waiting to accuse Jesus, waiting to see what he does. They had come to humiliate Jesus but he turned the tables on them. 'Which is lawful on the Sabbath: to do good or to do evil, to save life or to kill?' This was the big question. The Pharisees were there with all the law, presenting themselves as righteous people and yet they did not know the difference between good and evil, between life and death. In contrast, Jesus told the man to stretch out his hand, and healed him.

The man must have been surprised at Jesus' request. He was probably thinking: 'This is an impossibility. I have

25

been here all my life with a withered hand. I have been struck down with the palsy and you ask me to stretch out my hand. You ask me to stand up and come to the front.' Jesus did not touch him but he left him with a decision to make. He had a choice to make. He could either do what Jesus said and enter into the relationship, or go away. He stretched out his hand. His step of faith resulted in his hand being healed.

The Pharisees had watched this miracle, but what was their reaction? They went out to plot to kill Jesus. Their obsession with the law had taken them to the point that they could not see Jesus meeting someone's need. All they could see was someone contravening their tradition and they wanted to kill him. Notice they were not scared to break the law—'You shall not murder'—rather they were concerned about their interpretation of the law. Yet we are the same. If Jesus working in our lives contravenes our law we try to quench the Spirit and kill Jesus.

The Herodians were loyal to Herod and collaborators with Rome. They were the antithesis of the Pharisees, yet their opposition to Jesus united them. This always happens in the end. Regardless of cultural, social and economic background, people unite against Jesus. Jesus united people for him or against him. You cannot sit on the fence. If you are undecided you have decided against him. If you are thinking, 'Is he or isn't he?'—he isn't.

Jesus didn't make a video. He wasn't on TV. His PR was word of mouth. Word had got around about Jesus because he met people's needs. He didn't preach religion. He developed relationships.

*F*or he had healed many, so that those with diseases were pushing forward to touch him. Whenever the evil spirits saw him, they fell down before him and cried out, 'You are the Son of God.'...

Then Jesus entered a house, and again a crowd gathered, so that he and his disciples were not even able to eat. When his family heard about this, they went to take charge of him, for they said, 'He is out of his mind.' And the teachers of the law who came down from Jerusalem said, 'He is possessed by Beelzebub! By the prince of demons he is driving out demons.' So Jesus called them and spoke to them in parables: 'How can Satan drive out Satan? If a kingdom is divided against itself, that kingdom cannot stand. If a house is divided against itself, that house cannot stand. And if Satan opposes himself and is divided, he cannot stand; his end has come. In fact, no-one can enter a strong man's house and carry off his possessions unless he first ties up the strong man. Then he can rob his house.'

Mark 3:10–11, 20–27

The Jews said, 'We believe in God, we have Abraham as our father. We are descended from David.' But it was all legalistic and meant nothing. In contrast, even the evil spirits knew he was the Son of God. What a contrast. The Pharisees wanted to kill Jesus but the evil spirits recognized his authority.

It is interesting to think that if Jesus had accepted the praise and adulation of the spirits, it could have spelt a long life of popularity and success in the world but death to his purpose and mission. By accepting death as instigated by the Pharisees, Jesus Christ chose life and fulfilled his purpose and mission.

Mark's thesis is that Jesus is the Son of God (Mark 1:1; 8:29; 15:18). Even the evil spirits knew that he was the Son of God. Just saying that you believe in God is not enough. The question is: Do you have a relationship with God? Is it real? Is it vibrant or is it just a rule-keeping thing?

Everyone who knows Christ does so, not because they

wanted God, but because God called them. God first called you before you called him. Notice this—there was a choice to be made. He called you and then you came to him. You had to make a choice. Jesus calls you, but he will not bang your house down.

The law says, 'See you, you're not good enough.' Jesus call us into a vibrant living relationship with him. He calls us independently, individually where we are at. The law kills, but the relationship with Christ gives us life.

Look at verse 20. See also Matthew 12:23: 'All the people were astonished and said, "Could this be the Son of David?"' According to Matthew the issue was: Is Jesus the Messiah/the Son of David? Jesus' family thought he was out of his mind because here he was, the man who had lived in their house for thirty years and people were calling him the Messiah. His family said, 'No, no, no. We'd better sort this guy out. He is a great guy but if he has started thinking he is God then something has gone wrong.' So they went to take charge of it.

If the family don't know the answers, surely the teachers of the law will know, because they have been steeped in tradition and they read the scriptures day in, day out. The scribes were expected to know the Bible inside out. The teachers of the law who had come down from Jerusalem said, in effect, 'He is possessed by Beelzebub. He is a liar. He is a wise dude but he is doing a con trick and is telling porkies.'

Think about the claims he made: 'I am the way, truth, life… No one comes to the Father except through me.' The teachers said: 'OK but he is claiming and doing these things through the power of demons.'

Jesus was able to make the most profound truths simple by expressing them in everyday language, often in parables. 'How can Satan drive himself out?' That is why we have so many divorces—because the kingdoms are divided. The

Bible says a married couple become one flesh but the world says, 'No—stay individuals, be two fleshes.' That is why they are fighting against each other. If a kingdom is divided can it stand? Of course not.

But Jesus' words and actions demand a response. C.S. Lewis wrote:

I am trying here to prevent anyone saying the really foolish thing that people often say about Him: 'I'm ready to accept Jesus as a great moral teacher, but I don't accept His claim to be God.' That is the one thing we must not say. A man who was merely a man and said the sort of things Jesus said would not be a great moral teacher. He would either be a lunatic— on a level with the man who says he is a poached egg—or else he would be the Devil of Hell... You can shut Him up for a fool, you can spit at Him and kill Him as a demon; or you can fall at His feet and call Him Lord and God. But let us not come with any patronising nonsense about His being a great human teacher. He has not left that open to us. He did not intend to.

C.S. Lewis, Mere Christianity, © 1952, HarperCollins Publishers

To see Jesus as a great human teacher and nothing more is not a viable alternative. He wanted each and every one of us to stand before him having had the opportunity to make that choice: lunatic, liar or Lord. You have the same choice to make today. You cannot sit on the fence. It is a choice between life and death. To be undecided is still to make a choice. To be decided you have made your choice.

Mark 4

What are your ears for?

Again Jesus began to teach by the lake. The crowd that gathered round him was so large that he got into a boat and sat in it out on the lake, while all the people were along the shore at the water's edge.

He taught them many things by parables, and in his teaching said: 'Listen! A farmer went out to sow his seed. As he was scattering the seed, some fell along the path, and the birds came and ate it up.

'Some fell on rocky places, where it did not have much soil. It sprang up quickly, because the soil was shallow. But when the sun came up, the plants were scorched, and they withered because they had no root. Other seed fell among thorns, which grew up and choked the plants, so that they did not bear grain. Still other seed fell on good soil. It came up, grew and produced a crop, multiplying thirty, sixty, or even a hundred times.'

Then Jesus said, 'He who has ears to hear, let him hear.' When he was alone, the Twelve and the others around him asked him about the parables. He told them, 'The secret of the kingdom of God has been given to you. But to those on the outside everything is said in parables so that, "they may be ever seeing but never *perceiving, and ever hearing but never understanding; otherwise they might turn and be forgiven!"'*

Then Jesus said to them, 'Don't you understand this parable? How then will you understand any parable? The farmer sows the word. Some people are like seed along the path, where the word is sown. As soon as they hear it, Satan comes and takes away the word that was sown in them. Others, like seed sown on rocky places, hear the word and at once receive it with joy. But since they have no root, they last only a short time. When trouble or persecution comes because of the word, they quickly fall away. Still others, like seed sown among thorns, hear the word; but the worries of this life, the deceitfulness of wealth and the desires for other things come in and choke the word, making it unfruitful. Others, like seed sown on good soil, hear the word, accept it, and produce a crop—thirty, sixty or even a hundred times what was sown.'

Mark 4:1–20

Have you ever noticed that you have two ears, two eyes but only one mouth? God created us in these proportions for a reason. There is a tendency for us to give too much attention to the mouth. The key words in Mark 4 are: *listen*, *hear* and *understand*.

It is called the parable of the sower, but it is much more the parable of the soil. The focus is much more on the listener than the sower. The seed is the word of God which is scattered. It falls, according to Jesus, on four types of ground: the path, rocky places, among thorns, and on good soil. Jesus knew that all four categories were represented in the crowd.

Verse 9 is a funny statement: 'He who has ears to hear, let him hear.' What else are your ears for, if not for listening—for holding your sun-glasses or dangling your earrings? I think Jesus was implying that most of us are better at using our mouths than our ears. He knew, too, that most of us in church are only half listening. The crowd around him were just the same. Many of them were not listening properly.

When he was alone he explained it to the disciples. He told them the secret of God's kingdom had been given to them. The disciples show that they have got ears and have been listening by the fact that they asked him what it meant. They don't just listen but go to him and ask.

When I first became a Christian I was excited when I read the Bible but I had to ask God: What does this mean? There are so many people who are content to be spectators. They are on the outside, going to church, but they never get to the point of asking questions.

Parables to many are just kindergarten stories, just quaint stories with no relevance to a complex world. Yet the more you go into them the more you see that they are very relevant to the world. There are many simple parables, but they have the most profound message.

This parable is of great help to us in understanding what happens when people hear the gospel: 'some fell along the path, and the birds came and ate it up... As soon as they hear it, Satan comes and takes away the word that was sown in them.' This is the vast majority of the public. The message does not even penetrate their cerebral cavity. It bounces off like a ball. Satan comes and takes away the word. Because it is not received and acted on, the adversary takes it away. I can think of several top athletes who are in this group. They have heard the gospel. They might have grown up in Christian homes or gone to church but as soon as they hear the message, Satan keeps taking it away.

Others, like seed sown on rocky places, hear the word and are glad to hear it. But since they have no root, they last only a short time. When trouble or persecution comes because of the word, they quickly fall away.

I knew an athlete who accepted the message and was pumped up. He bought a huge Bible. At breakfast he would have his big Bible with him. He always had tapes of Christian music. He was so excited about Christianity. He became celibate, changed his lifestyle. He spoke at meetings. He was even talking about going to Bible college.

Now he is nowhere. Things went wrong and he fell away. Now he is as far away from God as he will ever be. God did not fulfil his expectations. He expected A then B. He thought, if I become a Christian I will be successful. I will run faster. It didn't happen, so he gave up. He had no root. It is a good object lesson.

Sometimes I worry about altar calls, when people are asked to stand up and say that they have just committed their lives to Christ. We invite people to make a cheap decision for Christ. We offer them a shallow Christianity, 'sign here, wear the T-shirt and you're on your way' Christianity. It is rooted in an inspirational message, not in the Word of God. When the first crisis comes, such people's faith is exposed: the shallowness is shown up.

Still others, like seed sown among thorns, hear the word; but the worries of this life, the deceitfulness of wealth and the desires for other things come in and choke the word, making it unfruitful.

Most Christians are in this category. All of us have commitments. We have to make a living. There is the temptation to have one's faith but subordinate it to other things like one's job. It can be a real battle. We can be so caught up with climbing the corporate ladder that we don't make time for God and our spiritual life. Speaking personally, I feel that I go in and out of this category.

Finally there is the good ground. These are people who are faithful. God is more than just a distant memory. God is part of their everyday life. God is a daily reality, there in the good times and the bad. Everyone knows these people are Christians. When God calls them, they are ready.

I was known as an international athlete because I did international competition. When the British Athletic Federation called, I was always ready. They could rely on my performance, they knew that I would keep in shape and not let the side down. I didn't need to run international competitions every day to prove I was an international athlete. I just had to be ready for the day I was called upon.

Even among the 'good soil' there are contradictions in lifestyle. We still need to recognize that we are sinners and that we will sin. In our circle of friends there are probably people who are not Christians but who realize that we have the truth. The message 'provides shade' for such people (verse 32). Sometimes we are called just to be there as a Christian witness.

Sometimes you do not see the results from your witness at the time. Other times it is years later when we find out what impact our words have had. Once after I visited a children's home, I received this letter:

Hi Kriss

I really want you to be encouraged in the things you do, especially the small. Roughly 7 or 8 years ago you went to a children's home in Winchester. All the kids made a fuss over you because you were famous except me. I was an angry youth with the kind of problems kids have in care. Despite the bad, deliberate reception I gave you, you managed to break through and showed me the love of God. I'm 21 now and have been born again 2 years. After leaving the kid's home I went back to the street and the crimes of darkness that go on in them—labelled a no-hoper, but then Christ shone his light into my life. I remember finding out you're a born again Christian and God reminded me of that day you came to my children's home where I was so lairy. You took me for a little drive up the driveway, let me get out and said 'Jesus loves you'—Now I know!!!

Keep shining!

CU in the Kingdom, love in Christ, Sarah

He said to them, 'Do you bring in a lamp to put it under a bowl or a bed? Instead, don't you put it on its stand? For whatever is hidden is meant to be disclosed, and whatever is concealed is meant to be brought out into the open. If anyone has ears to hear, let him hear.'

Mark 4:21–23

Jesus is saying: 'Don't hide your light.' The gospel shows sin in your life and in others. We are not to do things to be like the Pharisees, but to touch other people's lives.

'Consider carefully what you hear,' he continued. 'With the measure you use, it will be measured to you—and even more. Whoever has will be given more; whoever does not have, even what he has will be taken from him.'

Mark 4:24–26

In athletics, if one trains, one improves. I started running for the army and I finished getting medals in the World Championship and the Olympics. When I first started I had a modicum of talent but I needed people to motivate me. In Germany I joined an athletics club and started training.

The more I trained, the better I became and the more my confidence grew. I started training with the army, then I was county standard, I moved on to national standard and competed in national championships. I began to win those too.

But if I stopped training through injury or loss of motivation it was easy to lose confidence. I hold the British record for the 400 metres hurdles in 47.82 seconds but now, several years on, I couldn't run it in 55 seconds. When I was competing, I couldn't train this week then take next week off and go back to it, expecting nothing to have happened. In athletics one week off can lose you three weeks' fitness. It is the same in the Christian life. We need a daily walk with God.

You need to keep training and you need to be ready when he calls you. The measure that you use will be the measure given to you.

With many similar parables Jesus spoke the word to them, as much as they could understand. He did not say anything to them without using a parable. But when he was alone with his own disciples, he explained everything.

That day when evening came, he said to his disciples, 'Let us go over to the other side.' Leaving the crowd behind, they took him along, just as he was, in the boat. There were also other boats with him. A furious squall came up, and the waves broke over the boat, so that it was nearly swamped. Jesus was in the stern, sleeping on a cushion. The disciples woke him and said to him, 'Teacher, don't you care if we drown?' He got up, rebuked the wind and said to the waves, 'Quiet! Be still!' Then the wind died down and it was completely calm. He said to his disciples, 'Why are you so afraid? Do you still have no faith?' They were terrified and asked each other, 'Who is this? Even the wind and the waves obey him!'

Mark 4:33–41

In verse 33 Jesus explained everything. We need to spend time with Jesus so he can explain our life to us. We need to know Jesus better individually. We do this through prayer and reading the Bible.

Notice, in verse 36, that Jesus left the crowd behind. This is an important spiritual principle. Jesus did not follow the crowd or do things because everyone else was doing them.

When the storm came, Jesus was at peace while everyone else was flapping. Jesus was asleep. 'Where is Jesus when we need him?' the people were thinking. Do we feel that sometimes? We say: 'Lord, don't you care that I've lost my job, that I can't pay the mortgage, that everyone hates me?'

The disciples might have thought that they would get peace and tranquillity when they got away from the crowd, but in reality they got into a bigger storm. Sometimes I think my life was OK until I became a Christian. Now problems have started. But we only have fear when we don't trust God. The secret is that Jesus could not only control demons and human disease, but also controlled nature.

How would Jesus sum up your life? Without a doubt you fit into one of the four categories. When you heard the gospel how did you react? Did you allow Satan to snatch the word away before it had had any effect on you? Did you act on the word, make a good start only to give up when the going got tough? Or have you allowed blind ambition, the cares of the world, the pressure of living in the twentieth century to marginalize Jesus in your life? He is still there but no longer at the centre of things. Alternatively are you sold out for Jesus? Are you living your life for him and bearing fruit for his kingdom? Only you can answer that.

Mark 5

People or pork chops?

They went across the lake to the region of the Gerasenes. When Jesus got out of the boat, a man with an evil spirit came from the tombs to meet him. This man lived in the tombs, and no-one could bind him any more, not even with a chain. For he had often been chained hand and foot, but he tore the chains apart and broke the irons on his feet. No-one was strong enough to subdue him. Night and day among the tombs and in the hills he would cry out and cut himself with stones.

When he saw Jesus from a distance, he ran and fell on his knees in front of him. He shouted at the top of his voice, 'What do you want with me, Jesus, Son of the Most High God? Swear to God that you won't torture me!' For Jesus had said to him, 'Come out of this man, you evil spirit!' Then Jesus asked him, 'What is your name?' 'My name is Legion,' he replied, 'for we are many.'

And he begged Jesus again and again not to send them out of the area. A large herd of pigs was feeding on the nearby hillside. The demons begged Jesus, 'Send us among the pigs; allow us to go into them.' He gave them permission, and the evil spirits came out and went into the pigs. The herd, about two thousand in number, rushed down the steep bank into the lake and were drowned.

Those tending the pigs ran off and reported this in the town and countryside, and the people went out to see what had happened. When they came to Jesus, they saw the man who had been possessed by the legion of demons, sitting there, dressed and in his right mind; and they were afraid.

Those who had seen it told the people what had happened to the demon-possessed man—and told about the pigs as well. Then the people began to plead with Jesus to leave their region. As Jesus was getting into the boat, the man who had been demon-possessed begged to go with him. Jesus did not let him, but said, 'Go home to your family and tell them how much the Lord has done for you, and how he has had mercy on you.' So the man went away and began to tell in the Decapolis how much Jesus had done for him. And all the people were amazed.

Mark 5:1–20

As a high-profile athlete it is hard to remain humble, purely because everyone elevates you and tells you how great you are. Everyone tells you how much they would like to be like you. The only problem is that I know who I am. I think, 'Guys, you are off the pace if you want to be like me.' Of course, it is not being like *me* but being a bit more like *Jesus* that really matters.

With understanding comes humility. The more you know the more you find out that you don't know. That is certainly true in the Christian life. The more you know of Christ, the more you realize that you don't know.

Nowadays it is not in vogue to talk about demons. However some of the things that happen in modern society can not be explained except by evil, demonic powers or spirits. We talk on the one hand about how good and clever man is and yet we see destruction and inhumanity all around. I cannot explain how this can happen except by reference to powers of evil.

The man in the story in Mark 5 lived among the tombs. He had supernatural strength. He decided to hang out in the tombs and society decided that was the best place for him. In our society we may think that we have progressed from calling people 'demonized', but we treat tortured, vulnerable, problem-laden people in much the same way: go to Piccadilly Circus, King's Cross and see the people hanging around or go to the Embankment and see the people in their cardboard 'tombs'. Our society doesn't know what to do with these people so it lets them hang around in dark, shady places.

This guy was chained and fettered. This man whom nobody could control, this man who had no authority over him, saw Jesus. When he saw Jesus he ran to him and fell on his knees in front of him. Suddenly he saw hope. He recognized someone coming in the distance and ran and fell before him. He realized that Jesus could do something for him. Recognizing the magnitude of his problems, the man was prepared to come to Jesus. It is fascinating that the man was able to see so clearly who Jesus was when most of the people missed it.

Jesus spoke directly to the evil spirit and commanded it to come out of the man. Jesus was going to show his authority over demons. Then Jesus asked him what his name was. He answered 'Legion'. A Roman legion was 600–1,000 men. There were many, many demons. They begged Jesus not to send them out of this area. They were comfortable in the environment where they were, among the tombs, among dead bodies. They didn't want to go anywhere else. Mark says they asked to stay in the area, Luke says they asked that they would not be sent to the abyss.

The demons asked to go into the pigs. They preferred to

have the body of a pig than to be sent out of the region. It is hardly surprising that the demons did not want to leave the region. They realized that this was a happy hunting ground. The demons realized that these guys were so obsessed with making money.

Now we come to the destruction of the pigs. We may ask, 'Jesus, how could you do this?' The pigs were someone's property. How could Jesus send the evil spirits into the pigs? The first question is: What were the people of the region doing keeping pigs?

It is likely that the incident happened in the region of Gadara (see Matthew 8:28). What you need to know is that the Gadarene people were shepherds, the premier shepherds of Israel, yet they kept pigs. You need to understand too that pigs, according to the law of Moses, were unclean. The question is what a herd of pigs was doing here in the region of Gadara. I would venture to suggest that even though it was forbidden, it was a profitable market.

Things that are forbidden are the things that we want. They become delicacies. As a society becomes decrepit the delicacies are wanted more and more. The Gadarenes had become pig farmers, totally against their own traditions. Their philosophy was 'The end justifies the means.' Even though they were not supposed to keep pigs, because of the money involved they did it.

Notice, too, that it says Jesus allowed them to go into the pigs. They wanted a body. They needed to go somewhere. Jesus allowed them to go into the pigs. It may be that Jesus felt that here was a need for an outward sign of the reality of the expulsion of the demons. Jesus also used it to show that the people felt that the loss of the pigs mattered more than the healing of the man.

The people who were looking after the pigs went to the town and said, 'Hey guys, check this out. If you want some pork, you've dipped out. They just went down in the water. What are we going to do?' The people from the town came to see what had happened.

Remember the 'Iraqgate' affair, the sale of arms to Iraq? The government had rules and regulations and gave everyone the impression that they may not sell arms to Iraq. Yet behind our backs, they had been doing that very thing and letting arms go to Iraq. The people who were telling everyone that they couldn't keep pigs were probably quite fond of their pork chops. That is the way of the world.

When the people came and saw the man who had been healed, were they glad? No. Were they excited? No. Did they welcome him back into society? No. They were afraid. Of what were they afraid? Mark doesn't tell us, but I wonder if they were afraid of Jesus because he had destroyed their merchandise. Were they afraid of Jesus because he had shown control over the demons? Were they afraid that Jesus might do other things in their city?

Those who had seen it told the others what had happened to the man and told about the pigs. They said, 'Listen, I saw what happened. This guy came ranting and raving and saw Jesus and bowed before his feet. Jesus cast out the demons and sent them into the pigs and your pork went and got wasted by this man. Check this out. Now what are we going to do? Should we rejoice that this man is ready to re-enter society or should we be sad that we have no pork chops?' That was the dilemma. It is the same question for us: Are we going to be happy earning money and being in the world without reference to God, or are we going to rejoice about what God is doing in the world in our midst? That was the choice for the people then and it is still the choice for people today.

The people began to plead with Jesus to leave their region. The saddest part of the passage is that the Lord granted their request and left the area.

The choice is to be there among the pigs or to be in your right mind with Jesus. Many will be afraid because it is safer to be out there trading, safer to be in the rat race. It is safer to be going along with the crowd than to look different and come in with Jesus.

It always amazes me how we as a society are more fond of animals than we are of people. This man had had a terrible existence, he had been ostracized from society. This man lived among the tombs. Yet when Jesus heals him, the people are more worried about pigs than about him. It is the same in our society. There are so many people who are homeless, so many people who are ill and yet we are more interested in Red Rum's state of health.

Jesus says: 'Come on guys. Get it right. Don't stay there among the pigs.' Look at verse 17. The people plead with Jesus for him to leave the region. The people would rather have the pigs and the demons than Jesus. The people would rather have the man among the tombs than Jesus among the living. 'Get out of here, Jesus!' They were making a choice. It is the same choice for people today.

The man wanted to go with Jesus. He knew on which side of the water to jump. Jesus was the good shepherd. The sheep knew his voice. The man was the only sheep here who knew Jesus' voice. He, ironically, was the man that society had ostracized and had said was off the pace. Yet he was the one man who recognized Jesus. The Gadarenes were good shepherds who had gone bad. The man had been touched by Jesus and wanted to go with him. The crowd wanted Jesus to go.

Jesus told him to go home and tell all his friends. Remember the parable of the sower, or soils, from chapter 4? Jesus wants this man to be 'like seed sown on good soil, hear the word, accept it, and produce a crop—thirty, sixty or even a hundred times what was sown'.

Up to now, Jesus had told people not to tell anyone who

he was (what some theologians have called the 'messianic secret' in Mark's Gospel). Now Jesus changes and tells the man to tell everyone. Why? Because Jesus was never going to come back to this region. For this region, 'today was the day of salvation', perhaps the only chance they would have to hear the message.

The demon-possessed man wanted Jesus because he realized who he was. Later in chapter 5 Jesus heals a sick woman and raises Jairus' daughter from the dead. Jairus wanted Jesus because he realized who he was. The woman wanted Jesus because she realized who he was.

In this passage we read about a man who had an encounter with Jesus which changed his life. However there were also those who observed the incident, had the opportunity of an encounter with Jesus, but in the end were left quite unaffected by it. This passage has real relevance for us today. We face the same dilemma. Either you live with Jesus or with the pigs. Either you really recognize what Jesus has done in coming into your life or you are lost.

Mark 6

Hindered by unbelief

*J*esus left there and went to his home town, accompanied by his disciples. When the Sabbath came, he began to teach in the synagogue, and many who heard him were amazed. 'Where did this man get these things?' they asked. 'What's this wisdom that has been given him, that he even does miracles!*

'Isn't this the carpenter? Isn't this Mary's son and the brother of James, Joseph, Judas and Simon? Aren't his sisters here with us?' And they took offence at him. Jesus said to them, 'Only in his home town, among his relatives and in his own house is a prophet without honour.'*

He could not do any miracles there, except lay his hands on a few sick people and heal them. And he was amazed at their lack of faith. Then Jesus went round teaching from village to village.

Mark 6:1–6

A fantastic miracle had happened in Capernaum. Now Jesus was returning to his own country. His disciples followed him. There were people who followed him around, listening to what he had to say. They sat at his feet. They watched what he did.

When Jesus taught, people were amazed, and asked: 'Where did this man get these things?' Jesus went to his own town. Boom! He went into the synagogue. Jesus was speaking fantastic truth. He was speaking with authority, not like the scribes and Pharisees, not according to the traditions of the Pharisees. Jesus didn't have to appeal to higher authority. He just said, 'You have heard it said, but I say...'

The book of Proverbs says, 'The fear of the Lord is the beginning of wisdom, and knowledge of the Holy One is understanding' (9:10). Jesus knew the Father so he had understanding. Therefore he spoke with authority.

Understanding is one thing but wisdom is something else. Wisdom is the application of knowledge. It is useless to have knowledge unless you can apply it to your life. Head-knowledge is not enough, it has to get to your heart. When I became a Christian I spent a year building up my head-knowledge. I knew loads of facts and figures about Jesus Christ, but it wasn't until I said, 'Jesus come into my life; if you are really real, show me' that it went down from my head and into my heart. All of a sudden I was wise, not as the world counts wisdom, but as God does. All of a sudden I feared the Lord and that was the beginning of wisdom in my life—but I have a long way to go. One day, though, I will be perfect as I stand before him face to face.

You may have all that head-knowledge and come to church year in year out, but you have no wisdom if you do not apply the knowledge. But Jesus applied the knowledge. He did mighty works. He didn't just stand there pontificating about high and mighty things, he spoke with authority by his words and by what he was doing. So the people asked: 'Who is this man who can say such powerful things and perform such mighty works?'

The people asked, 'Is this not the carpenter?' I have to confess that I am not very skilful with my hands. I may run fast but that is about all I can do. If I put up a picture it never hangs straight. The people knew Jesus. They said, 'Is this not the carpenter? We know who he is. How can he do all these fancy things? Is he not the son of Mary?' That was very disrespectful. This was a patriarchal society. It would be normal to speak of him as the son of Joseph.

They were questioning the legitimacy of his birth. What they were saying was: 'Can we trust the bastard?' See John 8:19—'Where is your father?', or John 8:41. What they said was, in effect, 'We were not born of fornication, we know who our father is. You are a mother's boy. You don't even know who your father is. This is the carpenter, we know him. We know his brothers—one is a plumber, another an electrician. We know these guys. We know what they are like. We know his sisters—they are just ordinary human beings so how can he speak with such authority?' They were offended that Jesus could come and speak with such authority.

Familiarity breeds contempt. These guys knew Jesus when he was a little boy and as far as they were concerned he still was that little boy. They had not accepted that Jesus had grown up. They had not accepted that at twelve years of age Jesus was about his Father's business. Jesus knew the scriptures inside out. Jesus knew who he was. He knew where he was going, but these guys still saw him as just a little boy. They did not understand who he was. When he taught them, they were offended at him. The hardest people to witness to are members of your family because they know who you are.

If you become a Christian, your friends could be offended. They might think you are not the person you were. You have changed. Your priorities change. You may no longer want to do the things you did before. Your friends might feel that you are not as interesting as you used to be. That could be the price of being a Christian.

Mark says Jesus could do no miracles in the place where he grew up, because of the people's unbelief. Now if human unbelief could stop God doing something, what do you think it is like for us? If unbelief stopped Jesus doing mighty works, what do you think it does among us? We want our church to grow. What stops it? Unbelief—our unbelief.

How can an infinite God be limited by finite man? Unbelief stopped people being willing to be helped. Jesus could do no miracles because all these guys could think about was, 'We know who this guy is.' The only qualification for getting to know God is being willing. You have to get up and come forward when he calls you.

All Jesus could do was put his hands on a few people and heal the sick. If that is all Jesus could do, give me lots of it. We would be pumped up if it happened to us, wouldn't we? For Jesus that was nothing. He wanted to do mighty works.

Calling the Twelve to him, he sent them out two by two and gave them authority over evil spirits. These were his instructions: 'Take nothing for the journey except a staff—no bread, no bag, no money in your belts. Wear sandals but not an extra tunic. Whenever you enter a house, stay there until you leave that town. And if any place will not welcome you or listen to you, shake the dust off your feet when you leave, as a testimony against them.'

They went out and preached that people should repent. They drove out many demons and anointed many sick people with oil and healed them. King Herod heard about this, for Jesus' name had become well known. Some were saying, 'John the Baptist has been raised from the dead'...

The apostles gathered round Jesus and reported to him all they had done and taught. Then, because so many people were coming and going that they did not even have a chance to eat, he said to them, 'Come with me by yourselves to a quiet place and get some rest.' So they went away by themselves in a boat to a solitary place.

But many who saw them leaving recognised them and ran on foot from all the towns and got there ahead of them. When Jesus landed and saw a large crowd, he had compassion on them, because they were like sheep without a shepherd. So he began teaching them many things.

Mark 6:7–14, 30–34

Jesus sent them out in twos because two witnesses were needed to prove something under Jewish law. On your own, your witness wasn't enough. Two witnesses were needed to establish it. He gave them power over unclean spirits as a sign that they were from God. They were not to take things with them, for God was to be their provider.

God's word is a two-edged sword. On the one hand it is the gospel of salvation, on the other hand it is the gospel of judgment. Jesus can be your saviour but he will also be your judge. Jesus told the disciples to give the people the message, to let them know where they were. If they didn't accept the message the disciples shouldn't fight it. They should turn around and go. You see Jesus had two roles, saviour and judge.

The early Christians would not bow down to Caesar. They said there is no God but the living God. John the Baptist said it straight to Herod—'Herod you are out of order'— when Herod took his brother's wife, and it ultimately cost John his life.

The success of the disciples' ministry was in big contrast to Jesus' own ministry in his own town. When the disciples went out, many came and many were healed. Many demons were exorcised. The disciples reported back.

'Jesus, let us tell you what happened, we were pumped up, we healed people, we did fantastic things for people. Jesus you've got to listen.' When men go out and do something they come back pumped—yeah, high fives, they exaggerate it, embellish. 'The fish was *this* big.' 'Jesus, let me tell you what we thought and did.' Jesus listened and said, 'OK, yes, fine.'

Then he said, 'Come aside...' When Jesus, in Mark, says, 'Come aside...', he has something important to say (see Mark 3:13; 4:10). Jesus didn't really tell them anything. Rather he showed them a picture. When the disciples went out this had really been a test run. They had done some things wrong but Jesus doesn't say, 'Bad boys.' He says, 'Come away on our own.'

But rather than getting to a quiet place they find thousands of people there. The disciples were tired, excited and with much to say. When they got there and found loads of people there they must have been frustrated. Other people were in the way. The disciples may have been frustrated but Jesus' reaction was to be moved with compassion.

The disciples had done their ministry but perhaps without compassion. When I look at my own life I can put up my hand and say that I believe I have done many things for God because I have had to, because I have wanted to, for many other reasons but not really because I have been moved with compassion.

When I became a Christian I was on fire, Bible punching, boom, boom! I was telling you everything in your face. Then someone said to me: 'Kriss that isn't the way to do it. You have to hang back a bit, mind your ps and qs and don't upset people.' And as I grew a little bit older and wiser I thought: 'OK, maybe you are right.' Do you know what? I wonder if I was off the pace. I think there is a time to chill and there is a time to be on fire.

Jesus wants us to come forward with what we have and offer to him what we have. Jesus said: 'Just give me what you have and I will multiply it.' The disciples got into the boat. Jesus prayed. Every time Jesus prays in Mark there is a crisis point.

When we have any kind of success in our ministry there is always the temptation to become proud, to accept the glory for ourselves. We need to pray that God will keep our feet on the ground. Was Jesus praying: 'Help me not to succumb to the temptation to accept the glory now'?

It is so important when we do things for God, when we have success, when we have those mountain-top experiences, that we don't forget to pray. Pray for the people you have just done something for. Pray that God will keep your feet on solid ground.

Jesus said to them, in effect, 'You have had exciting times, but sometimes in my service there are going to be trials and tribulations. Persevering faith is what is needed. When you are working for me, it's going to be tough. It requires a lot of effort to get out of that cocoon before you become a butterfly. You need to persevere. But when you go through trials I will be with you.' Many other miracles happened but I bet the disciples never ever forgot that day.

As you go about your business answering the call of God, as you take your stand, you will have trials and tribulations. At times you will be ridiculed. At times Jesus is going to be standing back watching you fumbling left, right and centre, fighting against the elements, doing all things the wrong way. But in all of these things know this—Jesus is with you and will come in the boat before it capsizes. He will take care of you. He will be there for you. He will make sure you get across to the other side.

Don't be like Herod. Herod took off the head of the messenger, which showed he wasn't listening. Herod will stand before God and have to give an account of himself.

Right now perhaps God has been speaking to you. If so, listen, because one day you will stand in front of the creator of the universe. If you don't listen, all your life will pass by and you will perhaps look back to today as the last chance you had to accept Christ.

Jesus would like to get into the boat of your life. He wants to stand right next to you. He wants to quell the storms in your life. He wants to make sure you feel you have a place and a home with him. The challenge that Joshua put to the people of Israel still is relevant today: 'Choose this day, whom you will serve.'

Tradition

*T*he Pharisees and some of the teachers of the law who had come from Jerusalem gathered round Jesus and saw some of his disciples eating food with hands that were 'unclean', that is, unwashed. (The Pharisees and all the Jews do not eat unless they give their hands a ceremonial washing, holding to the tradition of the elders. When they come from the market-place they do not eat unless they wash. And they observe many other traditions, such as the washing of cups, pitchers and kettles.)

So the Pharisees and teachers of the law asked Jesus, 'Why don't your disciples live according to the tradition of the elders instead of eating their food with "unclean" hands?'

He replied, 'Isaiah was right when he prophesied about you hypocrites; as it is written: "These people honour me with their lips, but their hearts are far from me. They worship me in vain; their teachings are but rules taught by men." You have let go of the commands of God and are holding on to the traditions of men.'

And he said to them: 'You have a fine way of setting aside the commands of God in order to observe your own traditions! For Moses said, "Honour your father and your mother," and, "Anyone who curses his father or mother must be put to death." But you say that if a man *says to his father or mother: "Whatever help you might otherwise have received from me is Corban" (that is, a gift devoted to God), then you no longer let him do anything for his father or mother. Thus you nullify the word of God by your tradition that you have handed down. And you do many things like that.'*

Again Jesus called the crowd to him and said, 'Listen to me, everyone, and understand this. Nothing outside a man can make him "unclean" by going into him. Rather, it is what comes out of a man that makes him "unclean".'

After he had left the crowd and entered the house, his disciples asked him about this parable. 'Are you so dull?' he asked. 'Don't you see that nothing that enters a man from the outside can make him "unclean"? For it doesn't go into his heart but into his stomach, and then out of his body.'

Mark 7:1–15

Tradition is very important. Tradition is what gives a people their identity, culture, customs, all passed down over a period of time. I am a traditionalist. When I go around the world, people know that I am British because of the way I act and the way I talk.

But tradition can have a nullifying effect. It can make you inflexible, unapproachable. Tradition can put certain people in power and the rest of the people in chains. Jesus broke many barriers of the traditional ways that people saw things.

The Pharisees were traditionalists. They came to see Jesus, but they saw the disciples and were put off. Often people come to church to see Jesus and the first thing they see is you and me.

The Pharisees portrayed their view of God in rules, regulations and rituals. Whereas Christ wants you to portray

God in the way you relate to other people. The love that Christ has brought into your life should flow through you into other people's lives.

The Pharisees came to see Jesus, saw the disciples, and didn't like what they saw. The disciples were eating food with hands that were ceremonially unclean. Holding to the traditions of the elders, the Pharisees did not eat until they had washed their hands ceremonially. The Pharisees had developed a series of rules and regulations, like fences, around the ten commandments. The idea was to stop anyone breaking the ten commandments. The problem was that they became commandments in their own right. People began to worship the fences rather than the God they were meant to serve.

Six times Mark mentions tradition. The Pharisees asked Jesus why his disciples did not keep to the traditions of the law. You see they had a vested interest. It was this tradition that put the Pharisees in a position of power.

They were asking an insincere question and Jesus did not answer it. They hadn't come to seek Jesus or to learn from him. They had come to find fault. They wanted to impose their traditions on Jesus and his disciples. Jesus does not answer their questions.

Instead he quotes Isaiah to them. 'These people honour me with their lips, but their hearts are far from me. They worship me in vain; their teachings are but rules taught by men.' He calls them hypocrites and says, in effect, 'You are so busy having everyone follow your rules that you miss the heart of the message. My message is about relationships, about helping people. Your message is about rules and regulations.'

Jesus said, in effect: 'My guys are out there in the market-place doing the business, healing and so on. They are getting on with the job and getting their hands dirty. They haven't time to wash their hands thirty-nine different ways, as you want them to. You guys are so busy bathing that you never get to people. You deliberately stay away from people.'

The Pharisees had replaced the law of God with their traditions. They did it to protect their position. The Pharisees were in their ivory tower; Jesus' followers were in the market-place.

If you find that God is not answering your prayers, look at the motivation you have in coming to Jesus. The Pharisees did not come to Jesus to get answers from him, their motivation was to rebuke Jesus for not doing it their way. Jesus won't answer you if you come with a wrong motive.

What is your motivation? Is it for you? Are you worried about your social standing or is it really to enhance your relationship with him?

Then the disciples asked him—but they were sincere. They said, 'Jesus, we have lived our lives according to the tradition of the elders, what are you trying to say?' Jesus understands that they are asking with sincere hearts and he is going to answer their question. He is disappointed, though, that they have not already grasped what he is saying.

Do you remember the time that you asked God into your life, when you were really sincere? When you said, 'Jesus I don't understand. God, open it up. Let me know', and—boom!—he did! But do you remember a time before that when you asked: 'Well if there is a God why is there so much pain in the world? If you are just, why do you allow it?'—you know that sort of question that you threw up as a fence and he didn't answer you?

When I was speaking at a church once, I talked about how I wanted to have money and stuff but, when I got it, it didn't satisfy me. Afterwards a student came up to me and said, 'Well, Kriss, I've listened to what you had to say.' And he said, 'How can you reconcile your faith with having such a big car? If I was a Christian I would give half my money to the poor and do all the good things I could think of.'

But that guy hadn't come to hear about Christ. He had come to pick up some apologetic argument to strengthen his own position.

Whether you have £10,000, £100,000 or £1 million does not matter. God wants to know whether you are controlled by your money or your car. Before I was a Christian I was controlled by the desire to get all these things. Now I own material things, but they don't own me.

The Pharisees thought that being godly was about living a good life, being clean, following a lot of rules and regulations. There is nothing wrong with rules except when the rules become God and replace the relationship we have with one another.

Tradition enables people not to think: we have always done it this way and we will continue to do it this way. The Pharisees said: we do it this way because that is the way we have always done it. But Jesus made them think.

Tradition empowers a few and incarcerates the masses. Jesus sets us free and empowers us. I am liberated by what Christ has done in my life. I no longer have to follow the masses. Tradition can hem you in and lock you in.

Tradition encourages inflexibility and is opposed to change.

Jesus left that place and went to the vicinity of Tyre. He entered a house and did not want anyone to know it; yet he could not keep his presence secret. In fact, as soon as she heard about him, a woman whose little daughter was possessed by an evil spirit came and fell at his feet.

The woman was a Greek, born in Syrian Phoenicia. She begged Jesus to drive the demon out of her daughter. 'First let the children eat all they want,' he told her, 'for it is not right to take the children's bread and toss it to their dogs.'

'Yes, Lord,' she replied, 'but even the dogs under the table eat the children's crumbs.' Then he told her, 'For such a reply, you may go; the demon has left your daughter.' She went home and found her child lying on the bed, and the demon gone.

Mark 7:24–30

In verse 24, Mark brings us into a new section. Jesus is coming to the pinnacle of his ministry. The tradition of the Pharisees would have excluded this woman from having anything to do with God. This woman represents everyone who isn't a Jew. Up to this time, if anyone wasn't a Jew it was very difficult to become one. Jesus' message was for everybody. This woman, who represents all the non-Jews, came to Jesus and begged him to drive the demon out of her daughter.

In contrast to the Pharisees, she came and threw herself before Jesus and begged him to do something for her daughter. 'Jesus, Jesus can you do something for my daughter? Something is going wrong, she is full of evil. Can you help her out?' That is how Jesus wants us to approach him, with a contrite heart and a broken spirit. 'Blessed are those who mourn. Blessed are those who weep. Blessed are those who hunger and thirst.'

He wants us to come to him saying, 'Jesus, Jesus, Jesus, can you help me?' Don't come to Jesus with your philosophical ideas and notions, for Jesus knows all the answers. You can't trick Jesus or beat him for he knows it all. You might want to come to Jesus with all your funky ideas. He wants you to come like a child. A child says, 'Dad, I don't understand. Can you help me?' That is how we should approach God.

The woman came to Jesus and recognized him and realized what he could do for her. The Pharisees, steeped in their own traditions, who knew the Bible inside out, did not know who this man was. This woman heard that Jesus was in the vicinity. She wasn't coming to try out her influential ideas. She came because she knew that Jesus could help her. Did she go to the Pharisees? Did she go to the Sadducees? Did she go to the scribes? Not on her life she didn't! Tradition excluded her from that situation. But she had heard about Jesus and she rushed to him. She asked him. She begged him, 'Can you do something for my daughter?'

Jesus' reply must have surprised her. 'First let the children eat all they want,' he told her, 'for it is not right to take the children's bread and toss it to their dogs.' Can you imagine it? This woman has had the courage as a Gentile to come to Jesus, as a Greek to come to a Jew, she enters the room and throws herself on the floor and Jesus calls her a dog. If we understand the context we will see that what Jesus was articulating was true. Gentiles were considered to be dogs because they were outside the covenant relationship with God.

Jesus was acting out the principle of 'to the Jew first and then to the Greek'. Jesus was saying, 'Lady, not your time yet.' He is direct and firm. You can be sincere and still not receive the answer you want. But check this lady out for persistence. She is not going to be fobbed off. She really wants an answer. She is wise. Even if she is a 'dog', she realizes that even a crumb from Jesus is enough. The woman recognized something in Jesus that the Pharisees with all their education had missed—that Jesus had come for her too.

I have only tasted a crumb of what Jesus has done for me but that crumb was enough to change my life. I have many questions for Jesus and many things I cannot tie down, but that crumb he gave me was enough to change my life. One day I will have the whole piece of bread.

'Yes, Lord,' she replied, 'but even the dogs under the table eat the children's crumbs.' Jesus told her that for such a reply her daughter would be healed. She went home pumped up. Compare her approach with the Pharisees. She went home and found everything sorted out. Jesus was true to his word. The truth had set her free. Contrast that with the Pharisees' religiosity, rules and regulations that had everyone in bondage—not to God but to man.

Then Jesus left the vicinity of Tyre and went through Sidon, down to the Sea of Galilee and into the region of the Decapolis. There some people brought to him a man who was deaf and could hardly talk, and they begged him to place his hand on the man.

After he took him aside, away from the crowd, Jesus put his fingers into the man's ears. Then he spat and touched the man's tongue. He looked up to heaven and with a deep sigh said to him, 'Ephphatha!' (which means, 'Be opened!').

At this, the man's ears were opened, his tongue was loosened and he began to speak plainly. Jesus commanded them not to tell anyone. But the more he did so, the more they kept talking about it. People were overwhelmed with amazement. 'He has done everything well,' they said. 'He even makes the deaf hear and the mute speak.'

Mark 7:31–37

Some people—like the woman—come to Jesus of their own volition; others are brought to him, like this deaf man. His deafness is a physical picture of what was happening spiritually to the Pharisees. The man was physically deaf; they were spiritually deaf. Although they could speak about pseudo-religiosity, they had missed what really mattered. The physical picture helps us grasp the spiritual reality. You can bring a horse to water but you can't make it drink. You can bring a friend to Jesus but you cannot make the friend a Christian. All you do is bring them to Jesus and beg him to open their ears.

When you bring a friend to Jesus don't expect it to happen the way it did last time. Jesus does things differently. He meets people sovereignly, differently and at their own level. He touches them differently.

When I came to Jesus I had done all the reading and I just said, 'Jesus help me.' I was open like a child and Jesus helped me.

You know how it is when you are with a crowd of people, and you try to talk to them about Christ. The reaction is, 'Load of rubbish. On your bike. You don't believe all that rubbish.' Then when you get them on their own, away from their mates, it's all different: 'Kriss, I've often wondered, did Jesus really do that miracle...' They are open when they are on their own. Jesus understands that. You don't embarrass people in front of their mates. You get them away from the crowd and you can talk to them one to one. That is what Jesus did. He took him away from the crowd.

Jesus spat on clay. It was vulgar, it was unconventional but it was a powerful message. Jesus did this and the man began to hear and speak.

The deaf man and the Syro-Phoenician woman came to Jesus, recognizing that he had the answer and trusting him. That is what people need to know. Commitment precedes confirmation.

In athletics you need to commit to world-class training before you become a world-class performer. Imagine if I wanted confirmation first that I would become a world-class athlete before committing to training. You would rightly say that I'm out of my mind. These guys were committed to find the truth, then the truth was confirmed. St Augustine said, 'I believe *in order to* understand.'

So often people come from a rationalist background and they think they have to doubt, doubt, doubt. Our usual, 'modern' way of thinking finds its origins in Descartes, the French philosopher, who has been called 'the father of doubt'. People think you cannot believe something until you have doubted it first.

The Pharisees came to Jesus with wrong motivations. They had questions to ask but they wanted to catch Jesus out, not find out the answer.

You may have to come to Jesus not with your own preconceived ideas, not predisposed to doubt, but ready to trust. Come with the little you have and ask Jesus for more. Ask Jesus to turn your life round and show you the real meaning, where you are coming from and where you going.

God is good. He really wants to touch each and every one of our lives. He is not into rules and regulations. He is an active, vibrant God. He is as active today as he ever was. All you need is the courage to go for it.

The times when I have really grown in my own life have been moments of abrupt change. For example, I was in the children's home and then I joined the army: an abrupt change, but I flourished. In athletics, I changed from 400 flat to 400 hurdles: an abrupt change, but it transformed my career. Christianity hit into my life. Boom! An abrupt change, but I turned round in an instant and became a changed person.

Go for it today!

(1) Do you still not understand?

During those days another large crowd gathered. Since they had nothing to eat, Jesus called his disciples to him and said, 'I have compassion for these people; they have already been with me three days and have nothing to eat. If I send them home hungry, they will collapse on the way, because some of them have come a long distance.'

His disciples answered, 'But where in this remote place can anyone get enough bread to feed them?' 'How many loaves do you have?' Jesus asked. 'Seven,' they replied. He told the crowd to sit down on the ground. When he had taken the seven loaves and given thanks, he broke them and gave them to his disciples to set before the people, and they did so.

They had a few small fish as well; he gave thanks for them also and told the disciples to distribute them. The people ate and were satisfied. Afterwards the disciples picked up seven basketfuls of broken pieces that were left over. About four thousand men were present. And having sent them away, he got into the boat with his disciples and went to the region of Dalmanutha.

The Pharisees came and began to question Jesus. To test him, they asked him for a sign from heaven. He

*sighed deeply and said, 'Why does this generation ask
for a miraculous sign? I tell you the truth, no sign will be
given to it.' Then he left them, got back into the boat
and crossed to the other side.*

*The disciples had forgotten to bring bread, except for
one loaf they had with them in the boat. 'Be careful,'
Jesus warned them. 'Watch out for the yeast of the
Pharisees and that of Herod.' They discussed this with
one another and said, 'It is because we have no bread.'*

*Aware of their discussion, Jesus asked them: 'Why
are you talking about having no bread? Do you still not
see or understand? Are your hearts hardened? Do you
have eyes but fail to see, and ears but fail to hear? And
don't you remember? When I broke the five loaves for
the five thousand, how many basketfuls of pieces did
you pick up?' 'Twelve,' they replied. 'And when I broke
the seven loaves for the four thousand, how many
basketfuls of pieces did you pick up?' They answered,
'Seven.' He said to them, 'Do you still not understand?'*

Mark 8:1–21

Jesus moved to the Decapolis region. In chapter 6 Jesus
had fed 5,000. My first reaction to this passage was to
think, 'Gosh, aren't the disciples a bit slow?' They ask:
'Where will we get enough food?' In chapter 6, Jesus
showed that he could feed the people in a miraculous way.
The disciples were in a similar situation to the one they had
been in before.

The people had come to hear Jesus and had got carried
away. Either they had already eaten their lunch or they
hadn't brought any with them. Whatever happened, they
had been with Jesus for three days and had nothing to eat.
Jesus had compassion on the crowd. Yet the disciples
hadn't figured that Jesus could do the same miracle again.

Perhaps the situation was that the disciples did not take

anything for granted. Jesus dealt with many people on many occasions but he didn't usually do the same thing twice. He did different things for different people. The disciples did not presume that Jesus was going to do the same thing all over again. In fact Jesus wasn't going to do the same thing all over again. There are some differences.

You must not presume that Jesus is going to do the same for you as he has just done for someone else, that he is going to do the same for this group as he has done for that group, or even that he is going to do the same in this part of your life as he has done in that part of your life.

But Jesus had a plan. He only did what God told him to do and did it in the way God told him to do it. This time he asked the disciples, 'Where can we go?' Last time they went to the crowd and asked what the crowd had to offer. This time Jesus went to the disciples and said, 'What do you have to offer?' They said they had seven loaves. The 5,000 were probably predominantly Jews, the 4,000 probably mostly Gentiles (the feeding takes place in the Gentile region of the Decapolis) and they were not necessarily followers of Jesus, just people who came to hear him on this occasion. Again the disciples could have been forgiven for not expecting Jesus to get involved with the Gentiles in a real sort of way. In a sense, what Jesus was doing was saying to the disciples: 'You are my disciples, give me what you have and I will take that, and in turn give it to people who don't even know me.'

There are so many people in this world who turn their back on God, but God still blesses them on a day-to-day basis. Taking from his own resources, he provides the air that people breathe, the light that they see, the things that they have. We all like to think about what we can do and what we are doing for ourselves. In fact it is Jesus using of his own resources to bless people.

That is what is happening here as all this multitude are

sitting down, 4,000 in number—gentiles, sinners, saints, Jews, male and female, bond or slave. They have been fed here because they have touched Jesus and he had compassion on them. The people ate and were satisfied. That is what happens when we come in contact with Jesus.

Jesus had made sure that not only was he going to talk to these people about what he had on his mind, not only had he shown his compassion by healing the blind man in the previous chapter, but he showed that he was interested in each and every one of those people individually and sovereignly.

In the boat the disciples are arguing about whose job it was to bring the bread. Jesus asked them something like this: 'Why are you talking about having no bread? Do you still not see or understand? Are your hearts hardened? Do you have eyes and fail to see? And ears but fail to hear? Don't you remember when I broke the loaves for the 5,000 how many basketfuls you picked up? Do you still not understand? Getting bread is no problem. If you are really hungry I can get you fish as well. Are you still worried about the material things of life? Having been with me for two and a half years, are you still just thinking about your stomachs? Having seen the miracles that I have done time and time again are you still anxious for material things?'

I have to admit that I would have been exactly like the disciples. I am sure I would have said, 'What have I forgotten? What haven't I done?' I would have thought about all the contributions I had made to God in the last few weeks and wondered what I hadn't done properly. Was it my prayer life or my Bible reading? What Jesus was talking about was far more spiritual.

The Pharisees asked for a sign. Jesus wants us to ask questions of him. Remember, Jesus knows your heart, so don't ask questions unless you really want to know the answer. When I was totally exasperated in my search for

God, with all my reading and research, I came to a point of just shouting, 'Jesus Christ, let me know you exist because I really want to know', like a child going up to its father.

But what the Pharisees were doing was asking as if they already knew the answer. The Pharisees asked in a spirit of 'OK Jesus, I've had enough of your shenanigans, you are a carpenter's son, you haven't been to school, you have been walking about now for the past two and a half years. We know that the Messiah will show a sign from heaven.'

There was nothing wrong with asking for a sign. Jesus' answer was in effect: 'Were the 150 signs I have done not enough for you? Why then should I now do a special sign for you?' Remember the temptation of Jesus when he said, 'It is not good to test God' (Matthew 4). Jesus was saying we should avoid getting into the mentality of always putting God to the test.

It starts small: 'I don't believe God really loves me. If God really loved me he wouldn't let me get into debt. If God really loved me he wouldn't let me be estranged from my wife, he wouldn't let my child die. If God really loved me he wouldn't let me get hurt.' We constantly put God to the test in these ways. Beware—this can start very small and grow very easily.

A little bit of yeast can spread like wildfire. The disciples didn't understand what Jesus was saying. They only understood the material. It is the same in my own life. I have been with Jesus for nine years and yet how often do I catch myself thinking about the material, about my work, my friends, my family, thinking about what other people are going to say, rather than thinking about what God is going to say?

But Jesus wanted to tell the disciples something that was so important. He said: 'Beware. I am not going to be around too long. The time is coming when I am not going to be around any more. Beware of the yeast of the

Pharisees.' All they were thinking about was bread, but man cannot live by bread alone.

How many times does God want to speak to you or to me and we completely miscue and carry on talking about where we are at physically, about what our mortgage is doing, what our shares are doing? We completely miss the point.

Do you still not understand?

(2) Once I was blind but now I see

They came to Bethsaida, and some people brought a blind man and begged Jesus to touch him. He took the blind man by the hand and led him outside the village. When he had spat on the man's eyes and put his hands on him, Jesus asked, 'Do you see anything?'

He looked up and said, 'I see people; they look like trees walking around.' Once more Jesus put his hands on the man's eyes. Then his eyes were opened, his sight was restored, and he saw everything clearly. Jesus sent him home, saying, 'Don't go into the village.'

Mark 8:22–26

Jesus again shows that he doesn't do the same thing twice. He has healed blind people before but not in the same way. This time the man does not see properly the first time. Now I am sure that Jesus could have healed the man 'Boom!'

like that first time round. But for some reason he doesn't. Again he is teaching the disciples something. When Jesus touches you and me for the first time you do not see properly.

Just as the man at first did not see properly, so when we first become Christians, we do not see properly. What we do see is not properly focused. So Jesus touched him again and then he saw more fully. And so it is for us when we get nearer and closer and walk more often with Jesus, we see better. What we will see is that this picture that Mark has painted for us here, this healing of the blind man, is only a shadow of what Peter is about to find out.

There is a time in all of our lives when we are spiritually blind and we have to come to a position where we actually realize 'you are the Christ'. Physical blindness here shows us a picture of our spiritual blindness.

Christ could have healed the man just by saying, 'Be healed.' In this case Mark shows the healing happening in two stages, and that can happen to us, too.

I remember clearly when I came to know the Lord. I was 26 years of age. I was enjoying life. I was a successful person, I had money, a beautiful wife, a lovely family, a fast car, a nice house. I had everything I thought I needed to give me life. Really I was blind but I didn't know it. I was just doing the things everyone did. All of a sudden I started worrying because all the things I had were not making me happy. In 1986 I went to the Commonwealth Games and there on my bed was a Good News Bible. It was good news for me because I could understand what it was saying; it was in simple English that I could understand. I started reading about this guy in it, Jesus Christ, and I was really interested.

And it was as if Jesus started leading me by the hand as I read the book. It was talking to me about my spiritual life. I read it in two weeks but even then I was partly blind. I had a lot of facts. I had read all this about Jesus and I was convinced. This was the business. But I still had questions: Was this guy the real McCoy? Was he a real person or is it just a fairy story? It took nine months for Christ to keep on wiping my eyes until I got to a stage where I said to Jesus: 'Look I like what I've heard but I'm not really sure that you are there. If you really are who you say you are, come and speak to me. Let me know.'

That night I met Jesus. I had a vivid, vivid dream—a vision. In meeting Jesus I saw clearly. He had already led me by the hand and had healed me partially and I knew all these facts. All of a sudden I not only knew about him—I knew him and my facts turned to an experience. I had this living relationship with this guy and I was over the moon.

Next day I went running down the track and Roger Black, Daley Thompson and Moses were there—that's Ed Moses, not the biblical Moses! I said: 'Guys, I met Jesus last night and all of a sudden my life completely changed.' At first they thought I was completely mad but gradually they came to see that I had indeed changed.

I met Jesus and I saw. That is what happened to this guy. In a way it happened to the disciples too. The big question is: 'What about you? You've read this book so you have learned a bit about Jesus. You know about him but do you know him? Have your eyes been opened or are you still blind?' Let Jesus open them today.

(3) Identity crisis

Jesus and his disciples went on to the villages around Caesarea Philippi. On the way he asked them, 'Who do people say I am?' They replied, 'Some say John the Baptist; others say Elijah; and still others, one of the prophets.' 'But what about you?' he asked. 'Who do you say I am?' Peter answered, 'You are the Christ.' Jesus warned them not to tell anyone about him.

He then began to teach them that the Son of Man must suffer many things and be rejected by the elders, chief priests and teachers of the law, and that he must be killed and after three days rise again. He spoke plainly about this, and Peter took him aside and began to rebuke him.

But when Jesus turned and looked at his disciples, he rebuked Peter. 'Get behind me, Satan!' he said. 'You do not have in mind the things of God, but the things of men.' Then he called the crowd to him along with his disciples and said: 'If anyone would come after me, he must deny himself and take up his cross and follow me.

'For whoever wants to save his life will lose it, but whoever loses his life for me and for the gospel will save it. What good is it for a man to gain the whole world, yet forfeit his soul? Or what can a man give in exchange for his soul? If anyone is ashamed of me and my words in this adulterous and sinful generation, the Son of Man will be ashamed of him when he comes in his Father's glory with the holy angels.'

Mark 8:27–38

Chapter 8 is the centre of Mark's Gospel. Jesus and his disciples went to the town of Caesarea Philippi. This ministry started in Nazareth, went round the Sea of Galilee, up to Caesarea Philippi, the furthermost point in the kingdom of Israel. Christ has done so many miracles, the disciples finally get the message of what his purpose was.

On the road Jesus asks his disciples: 'Who do men say that I am?' Everywhere he's gone there are massive crowds and people are asking: 'Who is this guy?' The disciples answer: 'John the Baptist, some say Elijah and others one of the other prophets.'

In saying Jesus was John the Baptist they were not far wrong because John the Baptist glorified God in everything that he did and pointed to the coming Messiah. Similarly, Jesus was always giving God the glory. So they saw partially.

Elijah was one of God's greatest servants and Jesus was a servant, serving the people. He had compassion on the people and served the people. Because of the miracles people may have thought Jesus had come in the power of Elijah.

Then Jesus asked the disciples: 'Who do you say I am?' After all that had happened a light goes on in Peter's head and he replies: 'You are the Christ, you are who you say you are, you are the Christ.' Everyone else is talking about Jesus being a good man, a good teacher and a good prophet but Peter says, 'You are the Christ.' But we will see that Peter only partially understands what it means to be the Christ, just like the blind man, whom Jesus had touched. Peter only thought that being the Christ meant that Jesus was going to destroy the Roman army, the people who had the Jews in bondage.

Jesus then began to teach them that the Son of Man must suffer many things and be rejected by the elders, chief priests and teachers of the law. He would be killed and after three days would rise again. He spoke plainly about this. Peter took him aside and began to rebuke him. On the one hand Peter says 'You are the Christ' with all that entails. For us it is obvious that being the Christ means that he is to be Lord of our lives. Yet Peter wants to rebuke the one who should be Lord of his life.

Does that seem familiar? Has God said, 'I want you to do this' and you said, 'No, I want to do that'? Has God tried to show you something in your life but you said, 'No I want to do this'? How many times do I still try to rebuke Christ when he wants to do something in my life. How many times does God have to renew my vision to help me to see clearly?

Now these people whom Christ has been with for the last year and a half have finally got the message, or so we think, of who Christ is. 'You are the Christ—you have a purpose.' Even so they still miss his purpose.

He turned round and rebuked Peter saying, 'Get behind me, Satan for you do not have in mind the things of God, but the things of men.' Peter is to be commended for he saw who Christ was when others didn't, but he still did not understand. Just like the blind man was partially healed, so Peter only partially saw what it meant.

In what was Peter's highlight, his moment not quite of glory but a spiritual highpoint, when he was nearest to Christ, when he recognized who Christ was, he still got rebuked for thinking about men and not about God. He was still thinking about himself and about bread rather than about spiritual things.

And that was the problem. When Jesus was meeting men in his ministry, whether they were disciples, demon-possessed or people coming in to watch his many miracles, they were not thinking about the things of God. They were thinking about the things of men. This was the indictment Jesus was bringing on everybody around him.

He was saying, even to his disciples: 'You do not know

my purpose—you think about the things of men, not the things of God. I have come to serve, to suffer, to save. That is my purpose. I haven't come to be popular, to be accepted by the intellectuals in society, to be with you, Peter, to be your mate.' Peter was saying: 'Jesus don't suffer, don't die, don't go away, I know who you are—I want your company.'

I haven't come to have your company, I have come to suffer, I've come to serve, to seek and save the lost. And in fact that, too, is what you are going to have to do. Jesus illustrates that in verse 31. The Son of Man has been delivered into the hands of men and they will kill him. After he is killed he will rise on the third day.

They did not understand this saying and were afraid to ask him. Having seen Peter rebuked they were afraid to ask him what was his purpose. They still did not understand. They saw Jesus serve others, but still did not understand his purpose.

They came to Capernaum and he asked them, 'What did you dispute among yourselves on the road?' They kept silent because on the road they had disputed who would be the greatest. They'd been with Jesus eighteen months, seen Jesus serve people left, right and centre, and all that was on their minds was, 'We want to be the greatest.' They didn't understand he came to suffer, serve and save the lost. They thought: 'Look you're popular, you've got all these friends, all these intellectuals interested. Can I be number one in your gang?'

After I retired from athletics I was very, very busy. I had to try to get my physical life in order, to establish a new career. I needed to make some dosh. I wanted to make my family happy, make things happen. The rat race is a hard taskmaster. I heard God say: 'Kriss beware of the danger of falling into the same trap as the Pharisees. Beware of trying to please people. Beware of politics and religious leaders.

Beware of your business. Don't lose sight of who I am or what I have got for you or what I want you to do. Don't lose sight of your ministry.'

There is a real danger of being really spiritual on Sunday, feeling great to be at church with God's people but by Tuesday you are in the middle of work and doing all sorts.

In fact you are doing everything but what you promised the Lord. That was the problem for Peter and it is exactly the same for you or me. Don't become like the Pharisees, keeping all the rules but missing the point.

What good is it if we gain the whole world but lose our souls? We live in a selfish, permissive society. It is all about me, myself, I. Increasingly people are talking materialistically about the cars we want to buy, the holidays we want to have, the home we want to build, our dreams in the sky. We have all sorts of materialistic ambitions. Our children hear only about me and what I want. Where is the moral leadership and who will set an example for them? Yet we blame the children when it goes wrong.

Paul wrote to the Galatians: 'The one who sows to please his sinful nature, from that nature will reap destruction; the one who sows to please the Spirit, from the Spirit will reap eternal life' (Galatians 6:8).

If you sow to please the Spirit you will have eternal life. That is something we all need to grasp and understand. What really matters is that you sow to please the Spirit. How do you sow to please the Spirit? It is not just reading the Bible—though that is important—but some people who read the Bible are still far away from God. It is not just going to church—although I go to church and it is important to go to church. There are loads of people who go to church who are far away from God. It isn't just praying, for you can pray and still be far away from God. It is what you do with people. We need to serve one another as Jesus did.

As we reach the end of this crucial chapter in Mark's

Gospel, the same question remains to be answered: 'Who do you say that I am?' It is easier to answer the other question: 'Who do people say I am?' It is easier to distance ourselves and talk about what others think, what others say, to trade in second-hand opinions. But Jesus isn't satisfied with that. He asks you a direct question: 'What about you? Who do you say I am?' Can you say with confidence, 'You are the Christ' and accept the implications for your life?

Transfiguration

A nd he said to them, 'I tell you the truth, some who
are standing here will not taste death before they
see the kingdom of God come with power.' After six days
Jesus took Peter, James and John with him and led them
up a high mountain, where they were all alone.

There he was transfigured before them. His clothes
became dazzling white, whiter than anyone in the world
could bleach them. And there appeared before them
Elijah and Moses, who were talking with Jesus. Peter
said to Jesus, 'Rabbi, it is good for us to be here. Let us
put up three shelters—one for you, one for Moses and
one for Elijah.' (He did not know what to say, they were
so frightened.)

Then a cloud appeared and enveloped them, and a
voice came from the cloud: 'This is my Son, whom I love.
Listen to him!' Suddenly, when they looked round, they
no longer saw anyone with them except Jesus. As they
were coming down the mountain, Jesus gave them
orders not to tell anyone what they had seen until the
Son of Man had risen from the dead.

They kept the matter to themselves, discussing what
'rising from the dead' meant. And they asked him, 'Why
do the teachers of the law say that Elijah must come
first?' Jesus replied, 'To be sure, Elijah does come first,
and restores all things. Why then is it written that the

Son of Man must suffer much and be rejected? But I tell you, Elijah has come, and they have done to him everything they wished, just as it is written about him.'

Mark 9:1–13

Remember that the end of the previous chapter had Peter acknowledging who Jesus was. We also had Jesus rebuking Peter because, although Peter recognized who Jesus was, he wasn't prepared to listen to Jesus all the way. When Jesus started talking about prophecies, Peter had a problem with the sufferings of Jesus Christ. Peter thought, 'If you are the Christ, the Messiah, why do you have to suffer?'

Peter, like all his Jewish contemporaries, could not fully understand the suffering servant. They believed that the Messiah was going to be the person who was going to overthrow the Roman government. Peter was a product of his time. Just like we are products of our time. We live and grow nurtured in the environment and we take on board the things of this environment.

Peter was showing the classic signs of being brought up in a Jewish environment, looking for their saviour, for their king of kings, for the glory, the person who was going to have the government rest on his shoulders. Peter would have been familiar with the prophecy in Isaiah 9.

For to us a child is born, to us a son is given, and the government will be on his shoulders. And he will be called Wonderful Counsellor, Mighty God, Everlasting Father, Prince of Peace. Of the increase of his government and peace there will be no end. He will reign on David's throne and over his kingdom, establishing and upholding it with justice and righteousness from that time on and for ever. The zeal of the Lord Almighty will accomplish this.

Isaiah 9:6–7

This was the Messiah that the whole of Jewry was looking for. This guy would overthrow all the Gentiles, no longer would Israel be subordinate to the whims of Greece or Rome or anybody else. This was a Messiah that Peter and all his generation were looking for. It had been 400 years since the last prophet, Malachi. The Jews had been waiting all that time for the prophecies about the coming Messiah to be fulfilled.

Peter was a product of his environment. When Jesus said in Mark 9:1 'I tell you the truth, some who are standing here will not taste death before they see the kingdom of God come with power' that was it for Peter. Peter had no doubt that Jesus was the Christ. He had problems when Jesus started talking about his suffering. But now all of a sudden Jesus is saying: 'My kingdom is coming with power and glory and some of you guys who are standing here will not taste death before they see the kingdom coming.'

Peter thought: 'All right, this is it friends—I am going to see the kingdom in my lifetime! At least I hope it is me Jesus is talking about. Some of us here are going to see the kingdom of God.'

They are taken up to this mountain, six days after Jesus has said this amazing thing that they would witness the kingdom of God coming in power and glory. You can bet your bottom dollar that Peter and all his gang were thinking—'Boom ! This is it! We are going to see the kingdom of God with glory. We're going to kick the Romans out of our country.' Six days later three of them go with Jesus. These are those who are going to witness something extraordinary.

Jesus takes them up to the top of a mountain and when he gets them up there all of a sudden the veil that had hidden the Spirit of God was removed, all of a sudden they saw Jesus in all his glory, the glory of God that we read about in the Old Testament, the glory that Moses spoke about, the glory that all the prophets spoke about, brilliant white, coming from inside out. The glory of God. This signified the Old Testament authenticating Jesus.

And they saw the glory of God coming out of Jesus, and now the prophets come and authenticate exactly the same thing. Moses was there representing the Law. Moses, who had led the children of Israel out of bondage, out of Egypt, was there glorifying Jesus. Here was Elijah, the guy who called down the rain, the guy who stopped the heavens, who challenged the Baal and all the prophets, the guy who confronted the world—here was Elijah, representing the prophets, also giving Jesus the glory. So in a nutshell the Law and the Prophets point to Jesus.

Peter said to Jesus: 'Rabbi it is good for us to be here—this is great news! This is brilliant! Obviously we are the people to see your glory!' Let me tell you something—right now Peter is here! Peter's here—he's up on the mountain—you're down there, he's with Jesus, this is great, brilliant! Peter's enjoying it. 'I want to stay here, I want to be with you, I don't want anything else—I am with you Lord, this is fantastic.' He recognizes what's happened. Peter is on cloud nine. Peter believes now, the kingdom is coming—the second coming is here!

'Let us put up three shelters, one for you, one for Moses and one for Elijah.' He did this because he didn't know what to say, he was frightened. Why do you think Peter was frightened? Peter knew what was happening, he understood that God was coming. The background to this is God meeting Moses in the tabernacle (or 'shelter') in Exodus 40.

Peter was excited. Then a cloud appeared and enveloped him and a voice came from heaven, from the cloud. 'This is my Son whom I love—listen to him.' This is the Father now also giving glory to Christ. This is my Son, listen to him. Here we have the Spirit elevating Christ, we have the Law elevating Christ, now we have the Father elevating Christ. God was here.

Suddenly when they looked around they no longer saw anyone with them except Jesus. All of a sudden, all was gone, just Jesus. As they were coming down the mountain, Jesus gave them orders not to tell anyone what they had seen until the Son of Man had risen from the dead.

Now they kept the matter to themselves discussing what rising from the dead meant. What's he talking about—what is rising from the dead? Peter again starts stumbling over the same problem he had in 8:31–32 when he rebuked Christ for talking about suffering. Not just Peter, but James and John. And they asked him, 'Why do the teachers of the Law say that Elijah must come first? If we've just seen you in all your glory—why do we need Elijah?'

Jesus replied, 'To be sure Elijah does come first and restore all things, but why then is it written that the Son of Man must suffer much and be rejected?' Isaiah 53—read it and weep. Psalm 22—read it and weep. This is very important—Peter knew his scripture and he said, 'Lord what are you talking about suffering for? Elijah has to come first.' But Jesus combated that with scripture and said look at Psalm 22:6, 'But I am a worm and not a man, scorned by men and despised by the people' or Isaiah 53:3, 'He was despised and rejected by men, a man of sorrows, and familiar with suffering. Like one from whom men hide their faces he was despised, and we esteemed him not.' Read it and weep.

All of us come to the Bible with different perceptions. All of us come from the environment we've grown up in. So we take on board certain things. But the Bible is a whole Bible and we have to understand that we have to balance scripture with scripture. Jesus said, 'Peter, you understand the truth but you don't understand the full truth. Yes, Elijah must come but I must suffer also. Yes, the kingdom must come but I must suffer beforehand.'

John the Baptist came in the spirit of Elijah, to be a forerunner, preparing the way for Jesus (see Mark 1:2–4). The inference is that John came to fulfil that prophecy. Then we find that not only did he come but also that they did to him what it said they would do.

So Jesus said that some of them would not die till they had seen the kingdom come in glory. What that meant, then, was that the kingdom was ushered in by Jesus, that, as it said in Mark 1:14–15, 'Jesus went into Galilee, proclaiming the good news of God. "The time has come," he said. "The kingdom of God is near. Repent and believe the good news!"'

The kingdom was here, the kingdom of God on earth would be seen inside us. As we become believers we usher in the kingdom. But the end of all things—the fulfilment—is yet to come, when Jesus returns in glory. Right now we have this surprise of Jesus spiritually involved in us.

As Christians, each and every one of us has had a moment of transfiguration when we saw Jesus in all his glory. That moment when we were up near the mountain top and we looked up and the whole perspective of life was changed from being down there to being up here and we thought, 'Yes, Lord Jesus!' And we thought 'Great!' and we understood life from a whole new perspective. Every one of us as Christians can understand that. But that is not it. You can't just stay in your tabernacle up there.

The challenge rather is to come down the mountain and live out the Christian life. It will not be easy. Jesus called it 'taking up your cross daily'. We are to follow Jesus, to do what he wants us to, not what we want to. We are to stand for truth and right in a world where dishonesty, cheating, deceiving and making a fast buck are much more the order of the day. It isn't easy. It is very costly but ultimately following Jesus will lead you into eternal life. You won't get a better offer than that!

Mark 9 takes in the glory of the transfiguration and also some hard teaching from Jesus.

'If your hand causes you to sin, cut it off. It is better for you to enter life maimed than with two hands to go into hell, where the fire never goes out... And if your foot causes you to sin, cut it off. It is better for you to enter life crippled than to have two feet and be thrown into hell... And if your eye causes you to sin, pluck it out. It is better for you to enter the kingdom of God with one eye than to have two eyes and be thrown into hell'

Mark 9:43, 45, 47

As you read the Gospels you cannot escape the conclusion that Jesus and the Gospel writers thought that hell was a very present reality, as real as heaven itself. There are three references to hell in Mark, all in this chapter.

There is a heaven and there is a hell. You have got to be prepared to say these things. Jesus offended people. Look at John 8:44—'You belong to your father, the devil, and you want to carry out your father's desire. He was a murderer from the beginning, not holding to the truth, for there is no truth in him. When he lies, he speaks his native language, for he is a liar and the father of lies.' How do you sugar-coat that?

Jesus offended the people who mattered in society. If you believe, you have got to stand up and be radical. So often we want to be respected, to be liked. Jesus wasn't like that. He was in your face. When the time comes, we have got to be prepared to be like him. If someone asks a question, we have got to give the answer.

At the 1988 Olympics there was a group of on-fire Christians and we had a great time but then unbelievers started coming. Everyone was having a great time singing. Two girls came in. They enjoyed the singing. Then we got down to some Bible study and they said to me, 'There are many ways to God and if you say that God loves us he's not going to be that bad to us, is he?' I stood up and said, 'The Bible says that Jesus is the way, the truth and life. No one can come to the Father except through him. If you don't accept him you are going to hell.' Oh my word! You would have thought I had gone mad. How can you say such things? And they went out. I started feeling bad. Had I been too heavy? But Jesus wants us to tell people the truth. Of course the truth must be tempered with love. Jesus is unwilling that any should perish. 'God so loved the world that he gave his one and only Son, that whoever believes in him shall not perish but have eternal life' (John 3:16). Jesus loves you and wants to save you, but if you don't accept him, your sins will be upon your own head. There is only one way.

The letter to the Hebrews says: 'man is destined to die once, and after that to face judgment' (9:27). I believe that, on that great day of judgment, each human being will be called to give an account of his, or her, life.

I would describe heaven as being in the presence of God and experiencing the goodness of God. I would describe hell, in contrast, as not being in the presence of God, not experiencing his goodness and being aware that you are excluded from God's presence and goodness.

On earth many people experience God's benefits without being aware of it. They experience the sunshine, food, social contact with other human beings—all of which are God's gifts—without being aware or acknowledging that God is the source. Hell, for me, will be God withdrawing every gift and provision and leaving man to himself. What a thought! Everyone in hell who refused on earth to acknowledge God will, I believe, be aware of his existence and that they have missed out and are excluded from what he has planned.

Remember the story of the rich man and Lazarus in Luke 16? On earth the rich man had everything. But only after his death did he realize that it was all from God. His reaction was to want to go back and tell all his friends.

The reason that people will end up in hell is because they have not believed and trusted in Jesus and accepted the forgiveness that he offers. If God said to me, 'Kriss give me one good reason why you should go to heaven', all I could reply is, 'Because you said so. You said that if I believe in you, I would have eternal life. But if it depends on anything I have done, then it's time for me to fry. I haven't got a chance.'

But anyone whose answer is, 'Well, I've done good things, I've supported good causes and I did this great thing', it will be just filthy rags. As Isaiah said: 'all our righteous acts are like filthy rags' (Isaiah 64:6).

On the day of judgment, those who get into heaven will be just as dirty or sinful as those who do not. The difference is just that some have believed in Jesus and accepted his offer of forgiveness.

For me the reality of death, judgment, heaven and hell is motivation enough to want to tell other people about Jesus. How about you?

Mark 10

What money can't buy

As Jesus started on his way, a man ran up to him and fell on his knees before him. 'Good teacher,' he asked, 'what must I do to inherit eternal life?' 'Why do you call me good?' Jesus answered. 'No-one is good—except God alone. You know the commandments: "Do not murder, do not commit adultery, do not steal, do not give false testimony, do not defraud, honour your father and mother."'

'Teacher,' he declared, 'all these I have kept since I was a boy.' Jesus looked at him and loved him. 'One thing you lack,' he said. 'Go, sell everything you have and give to the poor, and you will have treasure in heaven. Then come, follow me.'

At this the man's face fell. He went away sad, because he had great wealth. Jesus looked around and said to his disciples, 'How hard it is for the rich to enter the kingdom of God!' The disciples were amazed at his words. But Jesus said again, 'Children, how hard it is to enter the kingdom of God! It is easier for a camel to go through the eye of a needle than for a rich man to enter the kingdom of God.' The disciples were even more amazed, and said to each other, 'Who then can be saved?' Jesus looked at them and said, 'With man this is impossible, but not with God; all things are possible with God.'

Mark 10:17–27

I am a fairly new Christian—I've been a Christian for about nine years—and the Lord took me when I thought I was in my prime, when I thought I was a man, the don and everything else. But he showed me that my life was very very hollow, shallow. Guys and girls, I had some money then, I had some fame then, but what God showed me was that all those things I had were inferior to the greater name of Jesus.

There was this guy who was rich. He had loads of money. He had the smart clothes. He had the platinum cards. He could buy anything he wanted—except eternal life. He could charge anything he wanted to a charge account—except eternal life.

In another Gospel we're told he was a ruler. This guy was a rich powerful ruler. That means he had people under his control all the time and he had the power of judgment— the power to say yea or nay, the power of the sword. This guy could tell people to do many different things, but one thing he couldn't tell them to do was to die for him. When it was his time to die, it was his time to die.

We are told he was young. This guy was a young dude, in the prime of life. He might even have been able to run faster than me—or maybe not me. But he probably was a real fit young chap. But he understood that the only thing his youth couldn't guarantee him was eternal life.

Even though he was young, he knew that one day he was going to die. Wise man! We have seen that 'man is destined to die once, and after that to face judgment' (Hebrews 9:27). There's one thing we all have in common—rich, poor, young, old, power or no power, one day we are all going to die.

So far nobody's got away with it. God's on a good wicket there—one on one, one hundred per cent, everybody that's come has also gone. The book of Isaiah says: 'All men are like grass, and all their glory is like the flowers of the field.

The grass withers and the flowers fall.' That is something so important that we need to get on board—each and every one of us has one thing at least in common, one common destiny—we are destined to die. As we are born so we're going to die. One day there's going to be two dates. One will signify when you are born and the other will signify when you die. And in between there will be a dash and that will signify your life. That will signify what you did with your life.

This guy came rushing up to Jesus because he understood this: 'One day I am going to die.' A really important question was on his mind. 'Good teacher, what must I do to inherit eternal life?' The important question! Because this guy realized one thing. That even though he had loads of money, even though he was a man of importance, even though he was young, he was going to face death.

What does Jesus say to him? 'Why do you call me good?'

Now can you imagine if you had that burning question you really wanted to ask Jesus, something really, really important—and then he says to you, 'Why do you call me good?' Could you imagine saying, 'Are you mad?' You say to him, 'I've come to you with a really important question, I want to know about eternal life and you start talking about semantics! I don't want to know the philosophy of goodness. I want to know about eternal life!'

Jesus says to this chap, 'When you come to me, do you recognize who I am? Because there is none good but God alone.' Jesus was saying either, 'I'm not good,' or 'I'm God alone.' He was asking: 'Do you recognize who you are coming to?' God could answer this question with authority. A good teacher could only approximate.

Remember the quotation from C.S. Lewis in chapter 3? 'I am trying here to prevent anyone saying the really foolish thing that people often say about Him: "I'm ready to accept Jesus as a great moral teacher, but I don't accept His claim to be God."' Lewis called such a view of Jesus 'patronising nonsense'. Jesus wanted to check where the ruler was coming from. Was it just a bland phrase or did he mean it?

What Jesus was saying was, in effect, 'There is none good but God alone. Either I am God or I'm no good. No one is good except God alone. You know the commandments—do not murder, do not commit adultery, do not steal, do not give false testimony, do not defraud, honour your father and mother.'

The guy says, 'Bingo! I've been doing that since I was a boy.' In Judaism you had a load of things to do if you sin. What Jesus said to him now was that he had to fulfil the second half of the Old Testament. What Jesus hadn't told him was about the first law: Love the Lord your God. Have no graven images. Have no idols.

Notice what he says beforehand—the guy says 'Teacher'. The first time he comes to Jesus, he says 'good teacher'. The next time he says 'teacher'. What is the rich young ruler saying? He's saying what a lot of people say— 'You're not God.' 'Teacher,' he declared, 'all these things I have done since I was a boy.'

John's Gospel begins: 'In the beginning was the Word, and the Word was with God, the Word was God.' As Jesus is the Word, that really means that in the beginning was Jesus, Jesus was with God, Jesus was God. And we beheld his glory, the glory of the only begotten of the Father, full of grace and truth. We here on earth saw Jesus among us, this God who became man and dwelt among us. Jesus actually declared that he is the 'I am' which was a title that only God can take—the Everlasting One, the Holy One of Israel.

Thomas—who, when told about the resurrection of Jesus, had doubted—when he saw Jesus' risen face, said:

'My Lord and my God.' Jesus claimed to be God. And Jesus' words to this young man meant 'I am God.' The young man said to Jesus, in effect, 'Sorry my friend, no you are not.'

This guy believed that he had kept the ten commandments. What this man had done was that he had kept religion to a T. So many of us are so good at keeping religion. But what Jesus said is that 'I don't want religion— I want relationships. What I want is relationship with you. I want you to recognize who I am and I recognize who you are. You are but dust, you will wither and die. I am God and I love you with an everlasting love.'

Jesus looked at this guy and he loved him and he said, 'One thing you lack. Go, sell everything you have, and give to the poor, and you will have treasure in heaven. Then come follow me.'

I once met a woman who everyone was praising— everyone said she was so good, everything she did was wonderful, everybody loved her, she was so kind to all people, good to animals. I thought this woman must be something fantastic. Boom, this woman was the business! She looked after the old, the animals, and butter wouldn't melt in this woman's mouth. I spoke to her husband and said, 'This woman is absolutely incredible.' He said, 'Yes she really is incredible—some-times I don't believe it myself.'

That evening I was sitting next to her at dinner. We were talking about business things and we got to spiritual things. All of a sudden she started bawling, she started crying. I said, 'What's up?' She said 'Lord Jesus forgive me.' I said, 'What for?'

She told me this story. She said, 'I was working in an old people's home as a nurse and one of my friends came in and she had had a stroke. I really loved this friend. She had said, 'If ever I become incapacitated will you help me to end my life?' Every time I went to see her I would remember these words. The stroke was such that in the end all she could move was her eyes. Every day I went in there her eyes would follow me and tears would roll down, and I knew she was accusing me because I knew she'd made me promise to end her life. I found myself going to the pills, taking them from the cabinet, coming towards my friend and the next thing I know was giving her the pills and I gave her the water. And all of a sudden she died and I was banging on her chair... Will God forgive me?'

All of a sudden I realized that this woman had only been playing at being good because she hadn't forgiven herself for killing her friend.

I don't want to justify what she did, but God is big enough for that too. God will forgive any sins that we confess. She was working at being really religious, doing all the things. She went to church, she helped old people, she did all these things, purely to try to cover up the sin that was within her.

Jesus has already done that. The same is probably true of this chap here. He was out there doing all the good things he could do, just to try to live up to what God wanted him to be—or what he thought God wanted him to be. And all God wanted was him to love God. All his heart, mind and strength. But the Bible says this: 'For anyone who does not love his brother, whom he has seen, cannot love God, whom he has not seen' (1 John 4:20). How can you love God and not those who are around you? So God gave us these two commandments to love him and our neighbour.

The man said, 'I have done it since I was a boy.'

Jesus said, 'One thing you lack. Go, sell everything you have and give to the poor and you will have treasure in heaven. Then come and follow me.' At this the man's face fell because he had great wealth. You see. God knew this man's heart and God knew that this guy's god was his money.

You know, I went through life really wanting to be rich. I went through life really wanting to be famous, really wanting to be successful. I still do! But this time I understand the perspective, because I'd got lots of money, I'd got fame, I'd got success and it didn't satisfy me. I was never happy. I had money but I wanted more. I had a car, I wanted bigger. I was international—I wanted to be the best. This guy, his money had become his god. And he couldn't do the one thing God asked him to do. God has never let me down. God has given me more, bigger, better, more than I could ever imagine. All he wanted was for me to deny myself and come and follow him.

You can't outgive God. This guy didn't know this. The man's face fell and he went away sad because he had great wealth. He had realized that he lacked, even though he had money and position and even though he was young, he lacked. He had come to God for something special and when God told him, he couldn't give it up.

Let me tell you a story from my own life about money. Once my manager came up to me and said, 'Kriss I've got you two races and there are good bucks involved.' He gave me the dates, 25 July and 1 August. The problem was that on 25 July I had agreed to preach at church and on the second date I had agreed to do something else, for TV. But when I thought about the races all I could see was dollar signs.

I spoke to God about it. He said, 'Kriss, you've an appointment on the 25th.' I said 'Well, yes, but I could get out of it.' God said: 'Kriss you've got an appointment on the 25th.' I heard what God said but I kept thinking about the dollar signs, about the mortgage I had to pay off. It was my last year in athletics, one of my last opportunities to earn that kind of money. So I rang my minister, Paul Finn and said, 'Paul I'm speaking on 25 July, do you know who is speaking on 18th?' Paul said, 'I am.' I asked if there was any chance we could do a swop. He said that would be no problem. So I thought, 'Yes, I can run the race and get that money and still speak at church.' God said, 'Kriss, you're out of order, but I'll let you speak on the 18th instead of the 25th. But you are serving money and not God.'

Guess what happened? The meeting with the lucrative race got cancelled. That experience showed me that although I read the Bible, prayed and witnessed occasionally, I wasn't all there as a Christian. The Bible says, 'You cannot serve God and money.' I realized that I was putting money before God.

The hardest thing in life is to admit that you were wrong. There are not many people prepared to say, 'I got it wrong.' The real risk-takers are those who are prepared to say 'I don't know all the answers', the people taking the real risk are those who are prepared to go back through their past, through their friends, through their teachers, through their family, and say 'I'm going the wrong way. Guys don't do it! This isn't the way to go.' This guy here wasn't able to take that risk, because this guy had a lot of money, a lot of power, a lot of things ahead of him. And he wasn't prepared to give up all those things he knew, to be embarrassed in front of the crowd, to pay the price that God had asked him.

What I want to say is this: I don't know if this guy ever twigged what Jesus had said to him or ever had the chance to come back again. This guy could have gone out and got knocked over by a number 9 bus (or number 9 chariot!). I don't know what happened to this guy. I don't know what'll happen to you. Even though this guy was loaded, he understood that money couldn't buy eternal life. He knew he could die young, but he wasn't prepared to take the risk of going back all the way through his life and saying, 'I've got it wrong.'

Are you prepared to take that risk? Do you know what that risk entails? Have you gone through life and understood that, no matter how much money you have, you need more? Are you one of the people who looks through society now and sees the devastation that sin has had in our society? If you look in the papers and see business, you see politics, you see royalty, so many examples of sin in our world today. Wars in Bosnia, rumours of wars in Africa, wars everywhere. Wars in your house. All as a result of sin.

Do you realize you are going the wrong way? Do you realize that each and every one of us is a sinner? Maybe you've been going to church regularly, doing all the right things, saying Hail Marys, I don't know what, praying ten times a day. And yet you talk about your brother, you curse your brother, you don't care for your brother. Do you realize you are going the wrong way?

Jesus said to this guy, 'Deny yourself and follow me.' It's already been done because 2,000 years ago a man, Christ Jesus, went to death on a cross. He stood there and gave his life, both for you and for me. The Bible teaches that he paid the price that we could not pay. He became a sin offering for us, that we should become the righteousness of God. This other chap went for self-righteousness, he wanted to do it his way, not God's way. There's nothing for you to do. What can I do to inherit eternal life? Nothing! It's already done. The apostle Paul says: 'if you confess with your mouth, "Jesus is Lord," and believe in your heart that God raised him from the dead, you will be saved' (Romans 10:9). The risen Jesus himself says: 'Here I am! I stand at the door and knock. If anyone hears my voice and opens the door, I will come in and eat with him, and he with me' (Revelation 3:20).

This guy, when he left Jesus, left undecided; and yet you know if he died that day it meant he was decided. If you're not for Jesus you are against him. You cannot sit on the fence. You cannot be what I call a 'mug rump'—that means sitting on the fence with your mug at one side and your rump at the other. If you are not decided, if you're undecided, you have decided. You are either for me or you are against me.

You've got to make the same choice.

Lend me your car

As they approached Jerusalem and came to Bethphage and Bethany at the Mount of Olives, Jesus sent two of his disciples, saying to them, 'Go to the village ahead of you, and just as you enter it, you will find a colt tied there, which no-one has ever ridden. Untie it and bring it here. If anyone asks you, "Why are you doing this?" tell him, "The Lord needs it and will send it back here shortly."'

They went and found a colt outside in the street, tied at a doorway. As they untied it, some people standing there asked, 'What are you doing, untying that colt?' They answered as Jesus had told them to, and the people let them go. When they brought the colt to Jesus and threw their cloaks over it, he sat on it.

Many people spread their cloaks on the road, while others spread branches they had cut in the fields. Those who went ahead and those who followed shouted, 'Hosanna!' 'Blessed is he who comes in the name of the Lord!'

'Blessed is the coming kingdom of our father David!' 'Hosanna in the highest!' Jesus entered Jerusalem and went to the temple. He looked around at everything, but since it was already late, he went out to Bethany with the Twelve.

Mark 11:1–11

Imagine the scene. You have just taken delivery of the latest model sports car. You are just having your Sunday lunch and afterwards you are going to ride through the town and show everyone your new car.

The colt was for a special occasion and it belonged to someone. Jesus was saying: 'The colt was prepared for a special occasion and I am it.' Two strangers turn up and say 'Give me the keys, we want to have a burn-up.'

How would you feel if some stranger asked to take your brand new, never-driven, just-delivered, locked-up-in-the-garage-for-a-special-occasion sports car? You didn't buy it for someone else to drive it.

It doesn't make sense unless it had been arranged. Perhaps they thought, 'I want to give this to the Lord.' Maybe, for example, they had heard that the king was coming and that he might want a car when he came. Maybe they thought, 'OK, I won't use it as I wouldn't want there to be food stains on the seats when the king comes.' In those circumstances, having been prepared, you might be willing to give up the keys to your sports car.

Do you think that any normal king who comes to you and says, 'I want to borrow your car' would say, 'and I'll bring it back tomorrow. When do you want it back?' No, kings took and didn't return. Once a king took your land it was his. Jesus was saying in effect, 'I am the king, this colt was prepared for me.'

Jesus had authority to go and drive a car that didn't belong to him, or ride the donkey that didn't belong to him. Another thing about this colt was that it had never been ridden before.

The colt would be afraid of the crowd. A brand new foal in the middle of a crowd of thousands of people coming to Jerusalem for Passover week singing and shouting about David and the kingdom and here was this brand new colt, with a guy on his back, that was never ridden before, this colt would normally be going crazy. But this colt, this donkey, accepts God on his back with all his majesty and walks meek and mild through Jerusalem. And Jesus is making a point here. You understand Jesus has walked many many miles before. I don't think Jesus really needed transport for the last two miles of the journey.

What does Jesus do and how does the colt react? The colt just let Jesus sit on him. A colt has to be broken in before it can be ridden, but here Jesus just got on to it. The colt didn't try to throw Jesus off its back, because the colt was prepared. The colt knew who was sitting on him. He understood that this was his special occasion.

The people recognized that Jesus was the Messiah, the king of kings and Lord of lords. They were prepared. You don't throw down your brand new Armani coat unless you know who is walking on it.

On this occasion Jesus accepted the worship. Jesus was fulfilling the Old Testament prophecy from Zechariah 9:9— 'Rejoice greatly, O Daughter of Zion! Shout, Daughter of Jerusalem! See, your king comes to you, righteous and having salvation, gentle and riding on a donkey, on a colt, the foal of a donkey.'

We read in 2 Samuel 5:6, 'The king and his men marched to Jerusalem to attack the Jebusites, who lived there. The Jebusites said to David, "You will not get in here; even the blind and the lame can ward you off." They thought, "David cannot get in here."' Similarly now the city was in the hands of the lame and the blind.

The people knew who Jesus was, but the Pharisees and chief priests did not. They were the blind and the lame. David came and conquered the city physically. Jesus conquered it spiritually, but they were not ready.

The colt was prepared, the disciples were prepared, the owners of the colt were prepared, the people were prepared, but not the temple and the religious leaders.

Sometimes people say to me, 'Kriss, come on, you don't really need that sort of stuff—that's for people who need a crutch to lean on. Christianity really isn't the real thing is it, Kriss?'

In a way they are saying that Christianity is for those who are lame or blind. In a way they have a truth there. The fact is that what they don't see is their own lameness and their own blindness. God came to us because we were lame and blind, we were going through life doing the things lame people do. Blind to the spiritual aspects of life, living just for the mind and for the body.

And it is true that when Jesus comes to Jerusalem it is the lame and the blind, those who have found daily life and work hard, who recognize him.

I went to see *Les Miserables* and really enjoyed it. It is about the lame and the blind and the people in this city, the rich and the poor. We have them among us and Jesus said we'd always have them among us.

Don't be offended when people say you must be lame or blind to need Christianity, because in fact that is the truth. It's when you appreciate your lameness and blindness that you can receive Jesus' healing and sight and that the blood of the Lamb (referring to his death and resurrection) can really wash you clean.

On this occasion Jesus decides that he wants to get his new donkey and ride into Jerusalem, making a really important point, fulfilling the prophecy in Zechariah 9:9. The donkey was prepared. The people on the way were prepared. Jesus goes into the temple in verse 11 to see if it is prepared.

The next day as they were leaving Bethany, Jesus was hungry. Seeing in the distance a fig-tree in leaf, he went to find out if it had any fruit. When he reached it, he found nothing but leaves, because it was not the season for figs. Then he said to the tree, 'May no-one ever eat fruit from you again.' And his disciples heard him say it.

On reaching Jerusalem, Jesus entered the temple area and began driving out those who were buying and selling there. He overturned the tables of the money changers and the benches of those selling doves, and would not allow anyone to carry merchandise through the temple courts.

And as he taught them, he said, 'Is it not written: "My house will be called a house of prayer for all nations"? But you have made it "a den of robbers".' The chief priests and the teachers of the law heard this and began looking for a way to kill him, for they feared him, because the whole crowd was amazed at his teaching.

When evening came, they went out of the city. In the morning, as they went along, they saw the fig-tree withered from the roots. Peter remembered and said to Jesus, 'Rabbi, look! The fig-tree you cursed has withered!'

Mark 11:12–21

He went to Bethany, which means 'the place of unripe figs', but when he looked at Jerusalem he wept. In Mark 1 he told people that the kingdom was at hand but the people were not prepared. This was Jesus' triumphant entry but he came not on a stallion but on a foal, a colt; he did not come on a charger, but on a donkey. The common people recognized him but the bigwigs didn't.

The next day as they were leaving Bethany Jesus was hungry. He had compassion on some other people who were once hungry—4,000 people he fed, 5,000 people he fed, with a couple of loaves of bread and some fishes. Jesus can do anything. If Jesus is hungry he can make— BOOM!—bread like that. But Jesus is hungry. Seeing in the distance a fig tree in leaf he found out if it had any fruit. This is the same Jesus who walked into a temple and some Pharisees were thinking some things and Jesus said, 'I know what you're thinking', and told them. Keep that in mind.

Jesus comes to the fig tree and found nothing but leaves because it was not the season for figs. He said to the tree: 'May no-one ever eat fruit from you again.' Now, some people can't believe that the Jesus they had heard of every now and then—gentle Jesus, meek and mild—could come out here and curse a tree because it hadn't any fruit when it's out of season. It doesn't make sense. This is the God of creation and he doesn't understand that he's created a tree that isn't going to provide fruit for another eight weeks and he curses it because it hasn't got what it shouldn't have on it.

There are some big trees which have the beginnings of figs which would grow in six or eight weeks' time. It doesn't taste very nice but if you are hungry it will fill the gap. And Jesus, seeing this tree full of these leaves, goes to see if there may be some of these really early figs that are unpalatable but will fill the gap. Another thing—if these things are not on the tree it means there will be no fruit on that tree in the summer. This is an unproductive tree.

So Jesus sees all this beautiful foliage and so much promise around there and goes and doesn't find the bud. And in seeing it he curses it because it is not ready for him. There are no seasons for Jesus. We have to be ready in season and out of season. Jesus can come to you tomorrow and ask you to do the thing for him—that day! The tree wasn't ready. This tree was looking good but it was out of shape.

It was breathing the air, taking the water, it was using the soil and all the nutrients, but it wasn't providing any fruit. At the time the Lord came the tree itself was not prepared.

The donkey was prepared (even though it was a 'brand new' donkey). But this tree was not prepared, so Jesus cursed it and said, 'May no-one ever eat fruit from you again.'

I think Jesus did this also to show something about the city he was about to visit. Jesus comes to Jerusalem and finds it unprepared for his visit. On reaching Jerusalem, 'the City of Peace', Jesus entered the temple and made a commotion. He began driving out those who were buying and selling there. He overturned the tables of the money-changers and the benches of those selling doves and wouldn't allow anyone to carry merchandise through the temple courts at all. Jesus enters the City of Peace. All is peaceful, everyone is going about their daily business.

What are they doing? On a special occasion like the Passover, you had to come to give your sacrifice and offering. It may be a lamb or a dove but it had to be unblemished. Now if you had brought your couple of pigeons in a case from Nazareth, with all that noise going on, one of the pigeons is going to scratch his feather or his claw or something. So in the end people stopped bringing their own things and came to Jerusalem to buy this stuff. The chief priests understood there was a market here so they invited the money-changers into, not the sacred Holy of Holies, but to the courts surrounding the temple. So in that temple you had bartering going on and it became a new economic system.

Jesus comes down here and sees the guys ripping off the peasants, the people coming to buy the goods. If you came here with money from Palestine or Arabia, you had to change your money. You had to buy something without a blemish.

Jesus enters the temple and sees people sitting at the temple and quotes Jeremiah: '"My house will be called a house of prayer for all nations"? But you have made it "a den of robbers".' This was not new. In the Old Testament we read how Eli and his sons were doing exactly what the priests were doing right now. They were fleecing the flock. It says in Samuel they were snatching the meat supposed to be sacrificed and taking it home and cooking it even before it had been offered to the Lord. Here are these people doing exactly the same.

The chief priests and teachers of the Law heard the commotion and began looking for ways to kill him. Jesus went into the temple and did what could warrant death, and in fact it did. Remember he came and did all the other stuff and they didn't do anything. People went from Jerusalem out to Nazareth when he did his healing, out to Canaan, out to Capernaum, but they didn't do anything. But when Jesus came to Jerusalem and did what he did in the temple, he signed his death warrant.

The fig tree had withered. Jesus said the word and the tree withered from the inside. This is indicative of us too, when we don't have a spiritual life. On the outside you may be looking well. You put your tie on, and your clothes and you've got the gold on and stuff. On the outside you're like the tree with all the leaves. But inside spiritually you're dead. And what Jesus said to that tree happened. The unfruitfulness, the barrenness of that tree was there evident the very next day because Jesus said that. And when he came into Jerusalem he judged each and every person who didn't accept him as Christ. He said that one day we will all wither and die. We know that. No matter how good you look now, one day the body will wither and die. This tree had no fruit, and when they came back next day it had withered and died.

God calls some people to the ordained ministry but he also calls some like he called the donkey. You may be a new Christian—well it was a new donkey. God can come and call you to something. Jesus might only use you once. Perhaps the donkey was only used once but what an important task, to bring Jesus into Jerusalem.

Each of us sins. Each of us has skeletons in the cupboard. Look at the fig tree. Jesus was born for salvation but now was the time for judgment. That happens to each and every one of us. People who don't accept Jesus will one day stand before Jesus and it won't be the baby that they will see. It won't be the king on the colt. It will be the guy who comes down from the Mount of Olives. The one we read of in Revelation on the white horse with a sword by his side. He is going to come back to judge the city.

The fig tree had leaves on it. It had the promise of fruit on it but when Jesus came it had no fruit. Like the fig tree there are many people around now who look good on the outside. They have the leaves, they've got the clothes but they are withering on the inside.

Then Jesus came to the temple. The temple was where the sacrifices were being made. The people there should have been waiting for the coming king but in there they were buying and selling, like they are doing now; the economy is going on. Jesus said this is supposed to be my place but you are here just doing merchandise. He came in judgment.

The corruption of the system was the same here. They worshipped the system but they did not recognize Jesus. Look at Jeremiah 8:7–9: 'Even the stork in the sky knows her appointed seasons, and the dove, the swift and the thrush observe the time of their migration. But my people do not know the requirements of the Lord. How can you say, "We are wise, for we have the law of the Lord," when actually the lying pen of the scribes has handled it falsely? The wise will be put to shame; they will be dismayed and trapped. Since they have rejected the word of the Lord, what kind of wisdom do they have?'

Greatness is not in earthly wisdom. The common people recognized who he was. Greatness is not in military power.

Greatness is not in great architecture. Jesus says that greatness is in serving the people. Jesus came to serve. That is the message throughout Mark: the leaders were supposed to be serving the people but really they were robbing the people, making them pay extra for doves for the sacrifice.

'*Have faith in God,*' *Jesus answered. 'I tell you the truth, if anyone says to this mountain, "Go, throw yourself into the sea," and does not doubt in his heart but believes that what he says will happen, it will be done for him. Therefore I tell you, whatever you ask for in prayer, believe that you have received it, and it will be yours. And when you stand praying, if you hold anything against anyone, forgive him, so that your Father in heaven may forgive you your sins.'*

They arrived again in Jerusalem, and while Jesus was walking in the temple courts, the chief priests, the teachers of the law and the elders came to him. 'By what authority are you doing these things?' they asked. 'And who gave you authority to do this?'

Jesus replied, 'I will ask you one question. Answer me, and I will tell you by what authority I am doing these things. John's baptism—was it from heaven, or from men? Tell me!'

They discussed it among themselves and said, 'If we say, "From heaven", he will ask, "Then why didn't you believe him?" But if we say, "From men"…' (They feared the people, for everyone held that John really was a prophet.) So they answered Jesus, 'We don't know.' Jesus said, 'Neither will I tell you by what authority I am doing these things.'

Mark 11:22–33

What does Jesus say? Big statement! Have faith in God.

We need to learn from this. Have faith in God. The faith is not in yourself, not in your abilities, but in God. Jesus is now entering the kingdom. In Mark 1:15 Jesus said: 'Behold the kingdom is at hand, repent and believe the good news.' Remember how they were singing about David and the kingdom in chapters 9, 10 and 11? When Jesus came in on this donkey that was fulfilling a Messianic prophecy. They all knew that the kingdom was being ushered in. But what Jesus was saying now was this—that Jerusalem is going to fall. This place which they all knew was going to be the seat of the kingdom. Have faith in God, my friends, when all around you doesn't go the way you think it's going to go. Have faith in God. If anyone says to this mountain, 'Move!', it will indeed move, but it will be because of your faith in God, not because you want it to.

It will be because it's God's will, not necessarily your will. Remember Jesus prayed 'Your will be done, Your kingdom come.' I think he was saying here, 'Yes I have come to usher in the kingdom, but have faith when you see Jerusalem torn down brick by brick. Have faith when you are persecuted, when people say all manner of evil about you, have faith in God. Ask God what his will is in your life, how you can indeed usher in the kingdom. Thy kingdom come. Thy will be done. But have faith when things all around you are not going the way you would have them go.'

I think Jesus was saying here, 'Pray and believe that you have received it and it will be yours. Pray in the kingdom of God. Not only this, pray to forgive your trespasses.'

God's will is that his kingdom comes. We must pray for the kingdom to come. We must also pray that we will not succumb to temptation. The disciples who had just been praising Jesus had to realize that Jerusalem was going to be ransacked and yet they must still have faith. The kingdom will still come but it won't be great because of the buildings, it won't be great because of military might and it won't be great because of its intellectuals, but because the people there serve one another. Pray that you do not fall into temptation, pray for those around you. When you see these things falling around you, have faith and pray.

Jesus came to serve. Those in his kingdom will be servants. The monarchy liked to be served. The monarchy liked to oppress. Earthly authority rules by fear and judgment. But now the time had come—God's judgment was at hand.

Pharisees said: 'Who do you think you are? We have got everything sorted out. We don't need your sort here. You are just creating havoc. How dare you come here?'

Jesus replied with a question about John the Baptist. Jesus wasn't just in the temple, he was in their face. The scribes and Pharisees reigned in fear that if the people followed someone else they would lose their power base. It is the same in business, if you do not spend your money the business world loses its power. That is why they advertise, to get you to spend your money. You people have the power. The scribes and Pharisees recognized that, and they were worried. If the people went with Jesus they would lose their power.

People with earthly authority are driven by fear and greed. The problem is that we are scared to buck the system in case we lose out. Instead we work the system. Jesus wasn't scared to take the system on. The motivation of the temple system was greed. The money-changers were more interested in making money than the religious aspects.

It was those who thought they weren't blind and lame, who were unprepared, who were defending the city. They did not want to acknowledge what was going on. Don't be offended when people call you blind or lame. Don't be offended when people say Christians are people who need a crutch. You have seen the light. You have recognized that the kingdom is coming. You have recognized that the kingdom of God is coming. You will be prepared when he comes again.

Mark 12

The vineyard and some questions

He then began to speak to them in parables: 'A man planted a vineyard. He put a wall around it, dug a pit for the winepress and built a watchtower. Then he rented the vineyard to some farmers and went away on a journey. At harvest time he sent a servant to the tenants to collect from them some of the fruit of the vineyard. But they seized him, beat him and sent him away empty-handed.

'Then he sent another servant to them; they struck this man on the head and treated him shamefully. He sent still another, and that one they killed. He sent many others; some of them they beat, others they killed. 'He had one left to send, a son, whom he loved. He sent him last of all, saying, "They will respect my son."

'But the tenants said to one another, "This is the heir. Come, let's kill him, and the inheritance will be ours." So they took him and killed him, and threw him out of the vineyard. 'What then will the owner of the vineyard do? He will come and kill those tenants and give the vineyard to others.

'Haven't you read this scripture: "The stone the builders rejected has become the capstone; the Lord has done this, and it is marvellous in our eyes"?' Then

110

they looked for a way to arrest him because they knew
he had spoken the parable against them. But they were
afraid of the crowd; so they left him and went away.

One day I was out walking my dog, Dillinger. We set off
down a county lane and Dillinger shot off through a hedge.
When he didn't come back I followed him. The place where
he had gone was all overgrown and wild but I could see a
house beyond.

I quickly felt uncomfortable. I knew that I was
trespassing. The hedge and the house both shouted,
'private property'. I felt I had been given access to
something that wasn't mine. As soon as I could I got
Dillinger and left.

It was the same with the vineyard. The people in it did
not own it. They were just renting it. That is true in a sense
of all that you think is yours now. In 100 years someone
else will be living in your house. The same is true of the
world we live in. We don't own it, we are just tenants.

Jesus was saying just that. God was the owner. He had
sent prophets to his people in the Old Testament to make
sure that everyone knew who the owner was. The apostle
Paul wrote: 'The wrath of God is being revealed from
heaven against all the godlessness and wickedness of men
who suppress the truth by their wickedness, since what
may be known about God is plain to them, because God
has made it plain to them. For since the creation of the
world God's invisible qualities—his eternal power and divine
nature—have been clearly seen, being understood from
what has been made, so that men are without excuse. For
although they knew God, they neither glorified him as God
nor gave thanks to him, but their thinking became futile
and their foolish hearts were darkened' (Romans
1:18–21).

So Jesus is saying that, just like the servants in the vineyard, humanity in general and the Jews in particular have no excuse for not knowing of God's existence and their responsibility to him.

The very air that we breathe, the food we eat and the light that provides sight, shout loudly about the owner of our 'vineyard' (the world). We cannot own these things.

In practice, however, like the tenants of the vineyard, the Jewish people rejected the message of the prophets and in some cases abused the prophets themselves. When God sent the Son, they crucified him. Jesus knew that the people were going to reject him but that ultimately the prophecy would be fulfilled: 'The stone the builders rejected has become the capstone.'

The Jewish leaders understood the parable and knew that he was speaking against them. True to the ending of the parable they 'looked for a way to arrest him... But they were afraid of the crowd; so they left him and went away.'

Later they sent some of the Pharisees and Herodians to Jesus to catch him in his words. They came to him and said, 'Teacher, we know you are a man of integrity. You aren't swayed by men, because you pay no attention to who they are; but you teach the way of God in accordance with the truth. Is it right to pay taxes to Caesar or not? Should we pay or shouldn't we?'

But Jesus knew their hypocrisy. 'Why are you trying to trap me?' he asked. 'Bring me a denarius and let me look at it.' They brought the coin, and he asked them, 'Whose portrait is this? And whose inscription?' 'Caesar's,' they replied. Then Jesus said to them, 'Give to Caesar what is Caesar's and to God what is God's.' And they were amazed at him.

Then the Sadducees, who say there is no resurrection, came to him with a question. 'Teacher,'

they said, 'Moses wrote for us that if a man's brother
dies and leaves a wife but no children, the man must
marry the widow and have children for his brother. Now
there were seven brothers. The first one married and
died without leaving any children. The second one
married the widow, but he also died, leaving no child. It
was the same with the third. In fact, none of the seven
left any children. Last of all, the woman died too. At the
resurrection whose wife will she be, since the seven
were married to her?' Jesus replied, 'Are you not in error
because you do not know the Scriptures or the power of
God? When the dead rise, they will neither marry nor be
given in marriage; they will be like the angels in heaven.

'Now about the dead rising—have you not read in the
book of Moses, in the account of the bush, how God
said to him, "I am the God of Abraham, the God of
Isaac, and the God of Jacob"? He is not the God of the
dead, but of the living. You are badly mistaken!'

Mark 12:13–27

The Pharisees had questions to ask Jesus but they were
not sincere questions. They were not asking because they
wanted to know the answers. They wanted to trick Jesus.

Were they trying to take the mickey out of Jesus or
talking against themselves? Is their reference to Jesus as
'a man of integrity... not swayed by men' another way of
saying, 'How can anyone talk with full integrity, and never
be swayed by public opinion, received ideas or traditional
concepts? Only God can pinpoint truth with unbiased
eyes'? Certainly they knew that their own agendas (social
and political) informed their interpretation and opinion of
biblical truth. The next question would highlight the
problem.

We have seen previously that when people had genuine
questions to ask, Jesus had infinite patience (see chapter

11). He had all day to explain things to the genuine enquirer. However he could see right through the Pharisees' questions and he treated them accordingly, ultimately telling them that they were badly mistaken in their approach.

On this occasion Jesus is confronted by an unlikely alliance, Pharisees and Herodians, the religious and the political together. At face value their question was a reasonable one, 'Is it right to pay taxes to Caesar or not?' but Jesus saw through it to their hypocrisy and trickery.

The Pharisees would have expected him to say that taxes should be paid to God not the Romans. The Herodians would have expected him to back the political powers that be. So by coming together the Pharisees and the Herodians reckoned that one of them would have been able to catch him out.

Of course Jesus was right. The money belonged to Caesar, as head of the treasury. Caesar loans us the money so that we might live, barter and exchange goods in our society. We ought to give to Caesar whatever portion he demands so that he can run his economic system.

Now all that Caesar demanded was a portion of your money in taxes so as to sustain the economy and therewith the society. But God wants more than that. God wants you (your might, your mind, your strength). God knows that if he has you, he has your money. Someone or something can have your money and not have you. The Pharisees and religious zealots were a case in point. They paid their taxes disgruntledly but had no intention of being a stable fabric in the Greco-Roman society. We can give a portion of our money to good causes (so as to appease our conscience) yet have no stake in the charity or plight of the recipient. One's effort and time is more costly than gold or silver.

Then another group of jokers, the Sadduccees, came up with another ridiculously contrived question about marriage. Jesus in effect says 'Guys, you are trying to trap me', and catches them in their own trap.

In my experience most people who argue about Christianity are like this—they are rationalists arguing a point of view, not because they genuinely want to know the answer to the question, but because they are proud of their own humanistic ideology.

I once took part in a debate at Cambridge University about the existence of God. Opposing me was the chairman or director of the British Rationalist Society. His whole mission in life was to try to persuade people that God does not exist. What a way to spend your life! What a tragedy! As we debated I don't think that he was listening to what I was saying. I don't think he was really interested in considering the evidence.

The debate revolved around the motion, 'This house believes that without God life is meaningless.' As far as I am concerned this is obviously true. We may ascribe meaning to life ourselves, but ultimately, if there is no God and no eternity, then life is an exercise in futility which will end in nothingness.

The whole point about the Sadducees is that they talked about philosophical issues, yet they knew neither the scriptures or God's power. How many times have I debated theological issues with people, only to find out that they have never read the Bible, let alone had an experience of God.

Jesus told them they were speaking from a position of weakness. Their own viewpoint was vain wisdom. The spiritual world differs from the material world in as much as 'there is no male or female'. Hence their argument could not be extrapolated into the spiritual realm. So many people have their own presuppositions and prejudices which prevent them from coming honestly to consider the evidence.

In two separate incidents in this chapter, Jesus was able to explain the kingdom of God but they were not willing to accept the message. Instead there wanted to trick Jesus with their clever questions. They had an opportunity to have Jesus explain to them the things of God but they didn't want to listen. Sadly, it is the same with so many people in the today's world. Jesus is still calling but they don't want to listen.

History through the eyes of faith

As he was leaving the temple, one of his disciples said to him, 'Look, Teacher! What massive stones! What magnificent buildings!' 'Do you see all these great buildings?' replied Jesus. 'Not one stone here will be left on another; every one will be thrown down.'

As Jesus was sitting on the Mount of Olives opposite the temple, Peter, James, John and Andrew asked him privately, 'Tell us, when will these things happen? And what will be the sign that they are all about to be fulfilled?' Jesus said to them: 'Watch out that no-one deceives you. Many will come in my name, claiming, "I am he," and will deceive many. When you hear of wars and rumours of wars, do not be alarmed. Such things must happen, but the end is still to come. Nation will rise against nation, and kingdom against kingdom. There will be earthquakes in various places, and famines. These are the beginning of birth-pains.

'You must be on your guard. You will be handed over to the local councils and flogged in the synagogues. On account of me you will stand before governors and kings as witnesses to them. And the gospel must first be preached to all nations. Whenever you are arrested and brought to trial, do not worry beforehand about what to say. Just say whatever is given you at the time, for it is not you speaking, but the Holy Spirit.

'Brother will betray brother to death, and a father his child. Children will rebel against their parents and have them put to death. All men will hate you because of me, but he who stands firm to the end will be saved.

'When you see "the abomination that causes desolation" standing where it does not belong—let the reader understand—then let those who are in Judea flee to the mountains. Let no-one on the roof of his house go down or enter the house to take anything out. Let no-one in the field go back to get his cloak. How dreadful it will be in those days for pregnant women and nursing mothers! Pray that this will not take place in winter, because those will be days of distress unequalled from the beginning, when God created the world, until now—and never to be equalled again. If the Lord had not cut short those days, no-one would survive. But for the sake of the elect, whom he has chosen, he has shortened them.

'At that time if anyone says to you, "Look, here is the Christ!" or, "Look, there he is!" do not believe it. For false Christs and false prophets will appear and perform signs and miracles to deceive the elect—if that were possible. So be on your guard; I have told you everything ahead of time.

'But in those days, following that distress, "the sun will be darkened, and the moon will not give its light; the stars will fall from the sky, and the heavenly bodies will be shaken." At that time men will see the Son of Man coming in clouds with great power and glory. And he will send his angels and gather his elect from the four winds, from the ends of the earth to the ends of the heavens.

'Now learn this lesson from the fig-tree: As soon as

its twigs get tender and its leaves come out, you know that summer is near. Even so, when you see these things happening, you know that it is near, right at the door. I tell you the truth, this generation will certainly not pass away until all these things have happened. Heaven and earth will pass away, but my words will never pass away.

'No-one knows about that day or hour, not even the angels in heaven, nor the Son, but only the Father. Be on guard! Be alert! You do not know when that time will come. It's like a man going away: He leaves his house and puts his servants in charge, each with his assigned task, and tells the one at the door to keep watch. Therefore keep watch because you do not know when the owner of the house will come back—whether in the evening, or at midnight, or when the cock crows, or at dawn. If he comes suddenly, do not let him find you sleeping. What I say to you, I say to everyone: "Watch!"'

Mark 13

Mark 13 is an example of apocalyptic literature—like Daniel or Revelation. It deals with the end times. It is symbolic and visionary. Not everything in it is to be taken literally. There are often bits of it that we find very hard to understand. It is very easy to be dogmatic about things and to be wrong in your interpretation.

In Mark 13 there is also a tension between different levels of future fulfilment. Some of the chapter was fulfilled in AD70 when the temple was destroyed. Other parts of the chapter refer to events which are still to come. It is not always easy to distinguish the two. However what I think is the most important thing that Mark is trying to say is that Jesus is the Lord of history. Jesus knows the beginning and he knows the end and everything in between.

As Jesus and the disciples were leaving the temple, they

were impressed. 'Jesus, what a fantastic building! What a monument to history. This is the bee's knees! Jesus, isn't it great?' Now we have to understand that temple worship was the centre of Jewish religion. Josephus, a contemporary Jewish historian, wrote about the temple and how the stones for the building came from all over the world. It certainly was an impressive building.

The disciples were just in awe of the temple and were saying, 'Jesus isn't this brilliant?' Don't forget too that Jesus had recently (Mark 11) gone in and cleaned the temple of all the bad worship, hypocrisy and those who were trying to make money out of the temple system. Jesus stopped them in their tracks with a surprising statement: 'Not one stone here will be left on another; every one will be thrown down.' Jesus was saying, 'Guys, don't bother with this building, for it is going to be razed to the ground.'

Jesus was challenging the established way of thinking, telling them that the temple, on which their belief structure was based, was going to be destroyed. Jesus was warning the disciples of the danger of reliance on any particular symbol of religion. The time was coming when the temple would no longer be there and the disciples would be exiled from Jerusalem. Jesus was wanting to get the message across to them that, in the new order, the church and worshipping God centred on the people not on a building.

There is a gap between verse 2 and verse 3 as they walk from the temple to the Mount of Olives and you can imagine the disciples walking along thinking 'What is he on about? The Messiah is supposed to come and build up the temple and Jerusalem and the nation. He is supposed to be the Messiah and yet he is talking about the temple being destroyed. I don't get it.'

So Peter, James, John and Andrew asked him privately when it would happen and what sign would there be that it was happening. Note the first thing Jesus said was 'Watch out that no one deceives you.' Jesus could have given two simple answers to their questions but he didn't. He gave them a long answer. The disciples, along with all the Jews, were eagerly awaiting the coming of the Messiah and all that that would bring, such as the destruction of God's enemies and the ushering in of God's kingdom. However Jesus needs to explain a lot of things to them. Jesus gives them signs, but not signs that would enable them to give detailed chronological predictions, just sufficient to keep reminding them that it was going to happen.

The disciples knew that the present world would pass away. They were living in this idea that the present world was not all that there was. Paul writing to the Corinthians shows the same expectation: 'What I mean, brothers, is that the time is short. From now on those who have wives should live as if they had none; those who mourn, as if they did not; those who are happy, as if they were not; those who buy something, as if it were not theirs to keep; those who use the things of the world, as if not engrossed in them. For this world in its present form is passing away' (1 Corinthians 7:29–31). The same point was made in 1 Peter 4:7 with the added expectation that the end of the world was imminent. 'The end of all things is near. Therefore be clear minded and self-controlled so that you can pray.'

There is much in this chapter that is hard to understand but I believe that there are six points that cannot be disputed. Let us look at them one by one.

First, *the temple will be destroyed*. This occurred in AD70.

Secondly, there will be *deceptions*. Throughout the ages there have been deceivers who claimed to be from God and who led astray some believers. Jesus warns his followers to be on their guard against such deceivers. Paul warns the Thessalonians to be on their guard against such deception.

'The coming of the lawless one will be in accordance with the work of Satan displayed in all kinds of counterfeit miracles, signs and wonders' (2 Thessalonians 2:9).

One particular deception was the view that the second coming of the Lord had already taken place. 'Concerning the coming of our Lord Jesus Christ and our being gathered to him, we ask you, brothers, not to become easily unsettled or alarmed by some prophecy, report or letter supposed to have come from us, saying that the day of the Lord has already come' (2 Thessalonians 2:1–2).

Thirdly, there will be *wars*. There have always been wars, but in our century there have been two big world wars and I believe that they are indicators that things are beginning to happen, and that the world really is in upheaval.

Fourthly, there will be *persecution* of Jesus' followers. The early Christians suffered persecution under the Jews and later from the Roman emperors. This persecution has continued throughout church history and is still to be found in some parts of the world.

Fifthly, there will be *betrayal*. Families betraying each other may not surprise us but in Israel or Africa the extended family is a real big thing so this would have much more impact for people used to the close-knit families.

Sixthly, somebody or something will be *the abomination of the desolation*, 'the abomination that causes desolation standing where it does not belong'. This 'abomination that causes desolation' is first mentioned in Daniel. 'He will confirm a covenant with many for one "seven". In the middle of the "seven" he will put an end to sacrifice and offering. And on a wing of the temple he will set up an abomination that causes desolation, until the end that is decreed is poured out on him' (Daniel 9:27). 'From the time that the daily sacrifice is abolished and the abomination that causes desolation is set up, there will be 1,290 days' (Daniel 12:11).

It is also referred to in Thessalonians: 'Don't let anyone deceive you in any way, for that day will not come until the rebellion occurs and the man of lawlessness is revealed, the man doomed to destruction. He will oppose and will exalt himself over everything that is called God or is worshipped, so that he sets himself up in God's temple, proclaiming himself to be God' (2 Thessalonians 2:3–4).

Daniel's prophecy was fulfilled in 165BC when Antiochus Epiphanes sacrificed pigs in the temple and again in AD70 when the Romans overran Jerusalem and put up the eagle standards of the Roman legions in the temple, but there is still a future fulfilment to come when the antichrist is revealed.

This is a very difficult chapter, very controversial. The question for us to ask is, 'What is Jesus saying to us?' I believe that Jesus' message to us from Mark 13 is that we need to be alert, to be ready. He warns us that all sorts of things are coming—wars, earthquakes, persecution. Jesus is saying, 'Don't let them distract you from the main function of serving me.'

The main thing that Jesus keeps saying is that all this is going to happen and we must be on our guard. We must be ready. That is a message to us as Christians to be ready for his coming for he can come to collect us at any time.

Six times in this chapter we are told to be ready, to be alert, to be on watch: 'Watch out that no one deceives you' (verse 5); 'You must be on your guard' (verse 9); 'So be on your guard' (verse 23); 'Be on guard! Be alert!' (verse 33); 'Keep watch' (verse 35); 'Watch!' (verse 37).

We are to live our lives as children of light, not children of the darkness. We are to hang on in there because we know that one day he is coming to collect us to take us to be with him for ever. Make sure that you are ready when he comes.

It could have been you or it could have been me

T hen Judas Iscariot, one of the Twelve, went to the chief priests to betray Jesus to them. They were delighted to hear this and promised to give him money. So he watched for an opportunity to hand him over.

On the first day of the Feast of Unleavened Bread, when it was customary to sacrifice the Passover lamb, Jesus' disciples asked him, 'Where do you want us to go and make preparations for you to eat the Passover?' So he sent two of his disciples, telling them, 'Go into the city, and a man carrying a jar of water will meet you. Follow him. Say to the owner of the house he enters, "The Teacher asks: Where is my guest room, where I may eat the Passover with my disciples?" He will show you a large upper room, furnished and ready. Make preparations for us there.'

The disciples left, went into the city and found things just as Jesus had told them. So they prepared the Passover. When evening came, Jesus arrived with the Twelve.

While they were reclining at the table eating, he said, 'I tell you the truth, one of you will betray me—one who *is eating with me.' They were saddened, and one by one they said to him, 'Surely not I?' 'It is one of the Twelve,' he replied, 'one who dips bread into the bowl with me. The Son of Man will go just as it is written about him. But woe to that man who betrays the Son of Man! It would be better for him if he had not been born.'*

While they were eating, Jesus took bread, gave thanks and broke it, and gave it to his disciples, saying, 'Take it; this is my body.'

Then he took the cup, gave thanks and offered it to them, and they all drank from it. 'This is my blood of the covenant, which is poured out for many,' he said to them. 'I tell you the truth, I will not drink again of the fruit of the vine until that day when I drink it anew in the kingdom of God.' When they had sung a hymn, they went out to the Mount of Olives.

Mark 14:10–26

Judas was an opportunist who took every opportunity to further his own career. He loved the things Jesus said and saw the opportunity to further himself in his career through his association with Jesus. He did well and Jesus appointed him as treasurer. Matthew the tax-collector might have been the more obvious choice, but Judas got the job instead of him.

Remember too that the Jews were looking for a Messiah who would overthrow the Romans. When Jesus began talking about his death or about his kingdom which was not a physical kingdom, he was talking about things that Judas didn't want to hear. That wasn't what Judas wanted the Messiah to do. Judas was in a position of power as treasurer, he probably wanted a powerful position in the new kingdom. He wanted to be in the cabinet in the new era after Jesus had thrown the Romans out. But all Jesus wanted to talk about was his death.

Judas was getting worried. He had staked his chips in the enterprise. He had invested everything in it. All of a sudden his leader was talking about defeat and death. Jesus was saying, 'My kingdom is not of this world' and Judas may have been thinking, 'Have I made the wrong choice?' When he hears the chief priests and Pharisees talking about looking for an opportunity to kill Jesus, he may have thought, 'Perhaps I'd better jump ship before this one sinks.'

Judas made his choice. He got money but I don't think Judas did it for money. Thirty pieces of silver was not a big sum. Judas was more likely to be thinking of his position: 'If you guys are going to be the ones to be with, I want to be with you and guess what, I'm the guy who can deliver him to you. And don't forget it for I'll be cashing in my chips later on.'

Judas was absent, away doing his stuff. Is it significant that Judas called Jesus 'Rabbi' (teacher) (verse 45)? Did he only want to follow him for what he could learn from him, not as his Lord? More importantly he comes to do his dirty deed in a cloak of friendship. He didn't want others to know what he was doing.

I think that is true in our lives too. When we want to do things that are not quite right, we shroud them in the good things. Judas kissed Jesus, trying to pretend that he was not going to do the evil deed.

Remember Judas was a disciple. He was one of the Twelve, he had a successful ministry. He was given extra responsibility, but even he had the ability to betray Jesus.

Jesus said that one of the Twelve would betray him. None of the disciples turned round and said, 'It's Judas.' It was not obvious to any of them that it was Judas. The most amazing thing was that they all said, 'Is it I?' They realized that it could be any of them.

'It is one who dips with me.' Either Judas is next to him

and Judas is dipping as he says this, or they are all dipping at the same time. If it is the latter meaning, then as he said, they would all realize that it could be them. First they are wondering 'Is it I?' Then when Jesus says it is one who is dipping, they realize that it could be any of them. If it is the former, Judas is close to Jesus in an intimate position and—BOOM!—is identified by Jesus.

In John 13 we read of Jesus washing the disciples' feet on this occasion. Peter said 'Hey, mate—no way! There is absolutely no way that you are washing my feet.' He is feeling a bit bullish and thinking, 'You are my king and my Lord, I'm not having you condescend to wash my feet' (they were probably a bit smelly).

Jesus insists and washes Peter's feet. Jesus says that he is washing the feet to provide an example of how we should be servants rather than trying to be the boss. Perhaps that was Judas' problem, that he wanted to be the boss. Remember, too, the incident when the disciples were arguing about who is the greatest (Luke 9:46)?

In John 13:24, Simon Peter asks John to ask Jesus who the betrayer is. They are all worried about it. Jesus tells Peter Satan has desired to have him. Jesus is saying, 'Peter it could even be you.' It is important for us to understand this. Look at the sequence:

Someone is going to betray me—'Who me?', 'Who me?', 'Who me?' It is someone who is dipping in the dish—'Who me?', 'Who me?' Peter said, 'No way Jesus, I'm going to be with you. Don't wash me, I'm clean, I'm ready to rock and roll for you any time you like.' Jesus said to Peter, 'Simon, Simon, Satan has asked to sift you as wheat. But I have prayed for you, Simon, that your faith may not fail. And when you have turned back, strengthen your brothers' (Luke 22:31–32).

Peter replies, 'Not me, Jesus, I am the man in the house.' Jesus tells him that he will deny him. Peter's reply,

'Jesus are you mad? Me, even if I have to die with you I will not deny you.' Guess what? Everyone chirped up, 'I won't deny you, Jesus.'

They all came to Gethsemane to pray. Jesus is distressed and asks the disciples to keep watch. He returns and finds them asleep. 'Did I catch you sleeping Peter, could you not watch for one hour?' Remember that Peter was saying earlier: 'Listen, mate whatever happens I'm with you, I'm in the house.' The disciples were not aware how important this moment was.

Speaking as a military man, I would suggest that what they should have done was let someone sleep for twenty minutes while two kept each other company. Set up a little rota.

Again Jesus told them to watch and pray but again he found them sleeping. They were embarrassed. 'Jesus I am really sorry but we were tired.' If they had really been aware of the time and the pressure, they would have been awake. People who have a relative in distress find that they can stay awake for seventy-two hours in a bedside vigil. The body gives you an increasing rush of adrenalin. When it really matters your body just keeps you awake, with a superhuman burst of adrenalin. It had been a long day, they had been preparing the feast and so on and when it really mattered they went to sleep.

Judas came with a gang and the disciples all forsook Jesus. When we read the passage, remember it could have been you and it could have been me. This was the disciples. When Jesus really needed them not only did they fall asleep but when the big gang came they were all out of there like a shot. I would like to say in Peter's defence that he did manage to cut someone's ear off. That is important because it shows that he did actually have the adrenalin that he should have had when he was failing to watch. He thought, 'Oh my gosh, I need to do something' and boom!

he cut off the ear and Jesus says, 'No don't do that' and Peter says, 'If I can't do that I'm out of here' and he runs away.

It could have been you and it could have been me. It happened to be the disciples.

Jesus has been taken away and brought to the Sanhedrin. Someone says to Peter, 'You also were with Jesus weren't you?' Peter replied, 'No not me, it wasn't me.' Peter was feeling very vulnerable. Peter was out of his environment. Peter was on his own. Peter was in a place that he didn't know. All of a sudden he is feeling very exposed. This is a defeated man. This is someone going through the throes of denying Jesus. It could have been you and it could have been me.

Look at John 18:15–16: 'Simon Peter and another disciple were following Jesus. Because this disciple was known to the high priest, he went with Jesus into the high priest's courtyard, but Peter had to wait outside at the door. The other disciple, who was known to the high priest, came back, spoke to the girl on duty there and brought Peter in.'

The verse is deafening by its silence. What really struck me was that John knew the Sanhedrin. He knew the guys with the power. When Jesus was lambasted, when all the people were bringing false charges against Jesus, John didn't say a thing. He kept quiet. He mingled in the crowd.

You can imagine it, people recognizing John and greeting him. John remains silent, just listening to what is going on. Jesus is getting all sorts of treatment but John doesn't say a thing. All the disciples denied Jesus. Peter did it in words, others just did the high knees out of here. John was deafening by his silence. When Jesus really needed his mates none of them were there. It could have been you and it could have been me.

I believe that towards the end of Jesus' ministry the disciples got carried away doing many things. They were great servants. They would say to Jesus, if you need someone to get things ready, I could do that for you. If you want me to be treasurer, I could do that for you. If you want me to go and preach, I could do that.

Remember the contrast between Mary and Martha in Luke 10. Martha was slaving away in the kitchen but Mary sat at Jesus' feet and paid her devotions. She listened to what he had to say. I believe that she was at Jesus feet so much, listening, when everyone else was running around, that when Jesus really needed her, she had intuition. She paid her devotions to Jesus when it really mattered.

There are several things we can learn from this incident. We need to have our own quiet times and devotions with Jesus. When we start getting so busy that we stop sitting at Jesus' feet, we miss those times when he really wants us. When Jesus said, 'Watch', I believe he meant us to watch too. Jesus told Peter that 'Satan has requested you but I have prayed for you'. We have to watch ourselves. We need to watch the situations we get ourselves into. I believe that Satan has requested each and every one of us. We need to pray—that we don't fall into temptation for temptation is around us, right, left and centre. And those times when we stop praying are the times when we fall.

When Peter was with the disciples he was bold, when he was with the group he was a big man. He could chop off the man's ear. With the group he was great. But on his own he was a frightened little boy: 'I don't know this man. I had nothing to do with him. I have never heard of the name before.' We need to be careful at those times when we are on our own. I think that is why we have the Church. That is why God said it is better for brothers and sisters to be together. We have to look after each other. Just as stone sharpens stone, so one Christian sharpens another.

When you are on your own you will deny the Lord. If you don't do it overtly like Peter, you will do it covertly like John.

You will mingle in the crowd and just be one of the people.

Beware of periods of darkness, when you think no one will see you—how you fill in your tax form. Beware of times of great confidence. Peter stood up and said, 'Not me Lord.' It is in those periods of great confidence when you think you have got it all buttoned down that you need to be careful. Take heed when you think you stand, lest you fall.

This time it was the disciples. Next time it could be you or it could be me.

Mark 15

Jesus, shaken but not stirred

*V*ery early in the morning, the chief priests, with the elders, the teachers of the law and the whole Sanhedrin, reached a decision. They bound Jesus, led him away and turned him over to Pilate. 'Are you the king of the Jews?' asked Pilate. 'Yes, it is as you say,' Jesus replied. The chief priests accused him of many things. So again Pilate asked him, 'Aren't you going to answer? See how many things they are accusing you of.' But Jesus still made no reply, and Pilate was amazed.

Now it was the custom at the Feast to release a prisoner whom the people requested. A man called Barabbas was in prison with the insurrectionists who had committed murder in the uprising. The crowd came up and asked Pilate to do for them what he usually did. 'Do you want me to release to you the king of the Jews?' asked Pilate, knowing it was out of envy that the chief priests had handed Jesus over to him.

But the chief priests stirred up the crowd to have Pilate release Barabbas instead. 'What shall I do, then, with the one you call the king of the Jews?' Pilate asked them. 'Crucify him!' they shouted. 'Why? What crime has he committed?' asked Pilate. But they shouted all the louder, 'Crucify him!'

Wanting to satisfy the crowd, Pilate released Barabbas to them. He had Jesus flogged, and handed him over to be crucified. The soldiers led Jesus away into the palace (that is, the Praetorium) and called together the whole company of soldiers. They put a purple robe on him, then twisted together a crown of thorns and set it on him. And they began to call out to him, 'Hail, king of the Jews!' Again and again they struck him on the head with a staff and spat on him. Falling on their knees, they paid homage to him.

And when they had mocked him, they took off the purple robe and put his own clothes on him. Then they led him out to crucify him.

Mark 15:1–20

The first thing chapter 15 tells us is that a decision has been reached: 'Very early in the morning, the chief priests, with the elders, the teachers of the law and the whole Sanhedrin, reached a decision.' As we look through the chapter we will see a number of people who had a decision to make. The first ones were the Jewish leaders.

The Jewish leaders

The Jewish leaders had reached a decision, but on what basis had they reached the decision? As early as Mark 3:6 we read, 'Then the Pharisees went out and began to plot with the Herodians how they might kill Jesus.'

The reason that the Pharisees were plotting emerges in chapter 2. Jesus taught with an authority that they did not have. So the authority structure that Judaism had was shaken—as well as stirred. These people thought they knew what was best for the social, religious and economic area of Palestine. All of a sudden this man whose parentage was dubious stood up and started doing things, challenging their authority and not going the way everyone else was going.

The Jewish leaders were shaken and stirred and they decided that they were going to kill Jesus. In 15:1 we read that they had reached the point of actually validating their decision.

Jesus is handed over to Pilate. Pilate asks, 'Are you the king of the Jews?' Jesus replies, 'Yes, it is as you say.' Apart from that Jesus said nothing else. The Jewish leaders had made their decision.

Jesus

The next person who had a decision to make was Jesus. Jesus was here standing in the dock, first of all in front of the Jewish people but now in front of Pilate. In Mark 1:15 Jesus said, 'The time has come… The kingdom of God is near. Repent and believe the good news!' Before that there was the voice from heaven confirming Jesus' ministry.

But now Jesus is here in front of his peers, his countrymen, the Romans and Pilate and Jesus has a decision to make: is he going to forsake the Lord or isn't he? In answering 'yes' to Pilate's question Jesus was taking on the mantle of David and all the prophecies of the Messiah.

Remember Mark 14:60? 'Then the high priest stood up before them and asked Jesus, "Are you not going to answer? What is this testimony that these men are bringing against you?"'

Jesus made his decision out of a sense of duty and of destiny. The Pharisees and the Jewish leaders had a decision to make. Their decision was made out of a sense of authority and they were going to hold on to it.

Pilate

The Jews came and asked Pilate if he would release a prisoner. Now Pilate had a decision to make. Pilate is faced with a man standing before him. Jerusalem is facing heady times. It is Passover. There has been a great influx of religious people. The authorities are all shaken, they are all stirred because the structure has been discredited, has been challenged by this man, Jesus.

As Pilate looks at Jesus he is impressed. He sees everything that he knows about a king. He sees a sense of authority and well-being. Kings are people who don't flap in situations. He sees Jesus here in command of himself when things are going wrong.

The only charge that Jesus has answered is that he is in fact the king. All the other charges, Jesus has not answered. Jesus has not said a thing. As someone once said, 'Truth needs no flower of speech.' By Jesus' silence he eloquently showed the truth of that one statement that he was the king. He answered nothing else. In the English legal system we have just disregarded the right to silence. Here Jesus exercised the right to silence with dignity.

Jesus said nothing except that he was the king. There is another saying: 'Eloquent silence is more powerful than eloquent speech.' Jesus, in saying nothing else, elevated the one statement by which he was to be judged.

Pilate looked at him and understood that he was there not because he was guilty of anything except for being who he was, a king. Pilate looked at him and understood that the Pharisees, Jews and Sanhedrin had only put Jesus in the dock because he threatened their authority and power structure.

Yet in all this Pilate looked at him, understanding everything, but wanting to please the crowd. We have seen how authority and our position in life can influence our decisions. We have seen how a sense of duty and purpose and direction can influence our decisions. Here we see how peer pressure, the desire to be part of the crowd, to be accepted in society, to keep hold of your political position, can affect your decision. Pilate needed to keep the people happy. His authority was in Rome but he needed to keep the people quiet. Even though he knew the truth, he was not going to follow his convictions. He decided to do what was convenient. He sacrificed Jesus for the common good.

In another Gospel we read that Pilate washed his hands. Here we read that he asked 'Why?' three times. He did not want to take the responsibility on his own.

The crowd

Pilate offers the crowd the choice between Jesus and Barabbas. The name, Barabbas, means 'son of the fathers'. Barabbas was a traditionalist. He had committed murder in a riot. The traditionalists were the ones who wanted the Romans out, who were waiting for the Messiah, their knight in shining armour. Barabbas is their champion, willing to commit murder for the cause. In contrast there was Jesus, last seen riding into the city on a donkey. The chief priests who were shaken, stirred up the crowd. They asked for Barabbas. Perhaps the crowd didn't know who they wanted, but by the time the priests had got round telling them that Jesus could not be who he said he was, the crowd were ready to shout: 'Crucify him, crucify him.'

Crowds are notorious. People behave differently in a crowd. In this crowd there would have been people who had seen Jesus' entry into the city, who had shouted 'Hosanna! Hosanna!' who had perhaps thrown down their cloaks, but once they got into the crowd, untruth prevailed. A crowd, by its very nature, renders the individual not responsible or at least with diminished responsibility. In a crowd we do not have to be answerable for our own actions.

I remember as a youngster going to the Notting Hill Carnival. I was having a great time listening to my music and so on. Then towards the end of the evening there was a sense of frustration because there were police every-where. I can remember running up and down the street like a madman, kicking over bins, knocking things down, pulling down stalls and so on, not because I wanted to do it, but doing it because everyone else was doing it.

I remember going to football at West Ham. We would be singing and chanting on the terraces and all of a sudden there would be people running and chasing after other people. Outside the stadium we would start knocking over ice-cream stands, hot-dog stands and doing crazy stuff. Again I was doing it only because I was in the middle of a crowd.

Søren Kierkegaard said: 'No individual is ever as cowardly as a crowd.' No one is ever as bold as when they are in a crowd. In the crowd it was safe to shout, 'Crucify! Crucify!'

Yet Jesus exhorts us to be responsible for our own actions. Paul tells us to 'continue to work out your salvation with fear and trembling' (Philippians 2:12), but there is a cost to that. We have to remember the words of Jesus: 'If anyone would come after me, he must deny himself and take up his cross and follow me' (Mark 8:34).

Jesus stood there on his own. He would have no dealings with the crowd. He wanted no help from the crowd. He could have saved himself. 'Do you think I cannot call on my Father, and he will at once put at my disposal more than twelve legions of angels?' (Matthew 26:53). But he told people he did not want a party, he did not permit any violence in his defence, he would simply be who he was.

The authorities knew how to manipulate the crowd and get them on their side. It is easy to manipulate a crowd by telling them a few porky pies and saying the things they want you to say, but Jesus was here, shaken but not stirred.

Look at what a crowd can do when they don't have to pull the trigger. Not one of the crowd would have had the courage or the conviction to stand in Jesus' place, to look at the world and say, 'Friends you are going the wrong way', to look at authority and challenge it in the way he did, to stand there and say, 'I am the way and the truth and the life. No-one comes to the Father except through me... the truth will set you free' (John 14:6; 8:32).

Paul wrote to the Philippians: 'I want to know Christ and the power of his resurrection and the fellowship of sharing in his sufferings, becoming like him in his death' (Philippians 3:10). Paul was going one way and the world was going the other. In following Jesus there will be times when we incur the wrath of our fellow men, because we are going one way when the world wants us to go the other. Jesus in that predicament was always shaken but not stirred.

If you want to know Christ and the fellowship of his sufferings you have to pick up the cross, deny yourself and follow him. The Pharisees' attitude to the trial reflected their own presuppositions about Jesus, wanting to preserve their traditions. Pilate just wanted to look after himself, preferring political expediency. The crowd were going to and fro depending on who was manipulating them at a particular time. One day each of us will have to give an account of what we do on earth at the judgment seat of Christ. As an individual you will stand there and you won't be able to blame anyone else.

You may be shaken by anxieties, but please don't be stirred to move away from God's will.

A certain man from Cyrene, Simon, the father of Alexander and Rufus, was passing by on his way in from the country, and they forced him to carry the cross.

They brought Jesus to the place called Golgotha

(which means The Place of the Skull). Then they offered him wine mixed with myrrh, but he did not take it. And they crucified him. Dividing up his clothes, they cast lots to see what each would get.

It was the third hour when they crucified him. The written notice of the charge against him read: THE KING OF THE JEWS.

They crucified two robbers with him, one on his right and one on his left, [and the scripture was fulfilled which says, 'He was counted with the lawless ones']. Those who passed by hurled insults at him, shaking their heads and saying, 'So! You who are going to destroy the temple and build it in three days, come down from the cross and save yourself!'

In the same way the chief priests and the teachers of the law mocked him among themselves. 'He saved others,' they said, 'but he can't save himself! Let this Christ, this King of Israel, come down now from the cross, that we may see and believe.' Those crucified with him also heaped insults on him.

At the sixth hour darkness came over the whole land until the ninth hour. And at the ninth hour Jesus cried out in a loud voice, 'Eloi, Eloi, lama sabachthani?'— which means, 'My God, my God, why have you forsaken me?'

When some of those standing near heard this, they said, 'Listen, he's calling Elijah.' One man ran, filled a sponge with wine vinegar, put it on a stick, and offered it to Jesus to drink. 'Now leave him alone. Let's see if Elijah comes to take him down,' he said.

With a loud cry, Jesus breathed his last. The curtain of the temple was torn in two from top to bottom. And when the centurion, who stood there in front of Jesus, heard his cry and saw how he died, he said, 'Surely this man was the Son of God!'

Some women were watching from a distance. Among them were Mary Magdalene, Mary the mother of James the younger and of Joses, and Salome. In Galilee these women had followed him and cared for his needs. Many other women who had come up with him to Jerusalem were also there. It was Preparation Day (that is, the day before the Sabbath). So as evening approached, Joseph of Arimathea, a prominent member of the Council, who was himself waiting for the kingdom of God, went boldly to Pilate and asked for Jesus' body.

Pilate was surprised to hear that he was already dead. Summoning the centurion, he asked him if Jesus had already died. When he learned from the centurion that it was so, he gave the body to Joseph.

So Joseph bought some linen cloth, took down the body, wrapped it in the linen, and placed it in a tomb cut out of rock. Then he rolled a stone against the entrance of the tomb. Mary Magdalene and Mary the mother of Joses saw where he was laid.

Mark 15:21–47

There were groups of people walking past. It was Passover so there was a lot happening in the area. The chief priests were there. Many of them would have known about Jesus and what he had done. However Jesus had not done things the traditional way. He had questioned the authority of the scribes, Pharisees and chief priests. He had questioned the way they had perceived and administered their religion. People were used to the way things were and now Jesus comes and says, 'There is a new way and I have come to usher it in.'

In the statement Pilate had put on Jesus' cross it said that he was their king, their Messiah. But the Jewish authorities were having none of it. They would say that if he was the Messiah he wouldn't be on the cross. If he really was who he said he was he would be down there with them. In fact they chose Barabbas instead of Jesus because he was more like what they expected the Messiah to be, someone who was strong, a white knight in shining armour rather than a man meek and lowly riding on a donkey.

The Jews would have been familiar with Isaiah 9:

'For to us a child is born, to us a son is given, and the government will be on his shoulders. And he will be called Wonderful Counsellor, Mighty God, Everlasting Father, Prince of Peace. Of the increase of his government and peace there will be no end. He will reign on David's throne and over his kingdom, establishing and upholding it with justice and righteousness from that time on and forever. The zeal of the Lord Almighty will accomplish this' (Isaiah 9:6–7).

This was their Messiah, the one who would break down the barriers, and kick the Romans out. It would be like in the days of David when they were conquering the lands around them—defeating the Philistines, Hittites and so on. That was their Messiah. Jesus, in contrast, was a young man who was with the poor, the sinners, the outcasts. He was doing everything but showing himself to be an astute political leader. For this reason passers-by could not accept that this Jesus could be the Messiah. For them he would need to come off the cross and prove to them that he was the Messiah like David.

Now it is important for us to understand that the one thing Jesus could not do was come off the cross. He had to suffer, the just for the unjust, the one for the many. It was for that precise reason he had come.

Some people say that Jesus never claimed to be the Messiah. Here isn't it interesting that the people who did not recognize him as the Messiah still said, 'He saved others but he can't save himself!' It was common knowledge that Jesus had healed the sick, given sight to the blind and done mighty works among them but the people wanted to see more proof. The people said, 'Come down from the cross then we will believe.'

In our society we look for scientific evidence. We must first see then we will believe. People say, 'Seeing is believing', yet we also know that at times our sight can deceive us. These people said exactly the same. If they saw they would believe. But faith means we must first believe and then we will see. Sadly because of their preconceived notions so many of them saw but still could not believe.

The centurion

Let us call our next witness, the centurion. The centurion makes an amazing statement. He said, 'Surely this man was the Son of God!' The centurion was a Roman soldier. He had nothing to do with the Jewish religion. The centurion is an impartial witness. He is a detached witness who observes the whole thing. And from his observations he came to the conclusion that this was the Son of God. The centurion is linked to Pilate. Pilate had said that he found no fault in Jesus. Pilate had allowed Jesus to be crucified to avoid a riot developing. He washed his hands and also put up the notice 'The king of the Jews'.

Let us imagine a courtroom scene. The barrister stands up and questions the witness:

Barrister: *Mr Centurion, were you on duty in Jerusalem when Jesus of Nazareth was crucified?*

Centurion: *I was.*

Barrister: *Were you present at the crucifixion?*

Centurion: *I was. The execution was carried out by men under my command.*

Barrister: You stated that this Jesus was the Son of God. How did you come to that opinion?

Centurion: Well gov, what happened was this. I had a good night's sleep because I knew I was going to be on duty next day. There was a lot of commotion going on at the time. We were afraid there was going to be a riot, because of this Jesus who, I was told, thought he was a king. So I made sure I was ready for what was likely to be a difficult day when this Jesus was crucified.

In the morning some of my colleagues told me about the great evening's sport they had had with this guy. They had first all whipped him, with thirty-nine lashes, ripping the flesh off his bones, leaving him bleeding. To be honest I've seen men die after such beatings. If that wasn't enough, my friend told me, they dressed him up, put a royal robe on him and somebody made him a crown of sharp thorns.

Then apparently the soldiers blindfolded him, took turns to smack him in the mouth and made him guess which one had hit him. The funny thing was that he remained calm and hardly said a thing. When they had had enough, they sent him out to be crucified. The thing that surprised me was that though he was supposed to be a king, there was no one around to carry the cross for him.

So we had to drag a guy out of the crowd—a slave from North Africa—to carry the cross for him, as nobody else was prepared to do it for him. What impressed me was how quiet and calm this Jesus fellow was. He wasn't squealing for mercy. He didn't renege on his claims even though no one was on his side, not even his friends. I watched as my men nailed him to the cross—hands and feet—and even then he did not squeal. People were insulting him, his fellow-countrymen, even the religious leaders were having a go. I looked at his eyes and he *seemed so calm and tranquil as if this was supposed to be.*

I continued to stand beside the cross and couldn't help overhearing his conversation with the other two who were being crucified. One of them abused him and he just forgave him and he actually said to the other one that he would go with him where he was going after death. Then all of a sudden something incredible happened. It was high noon, the sun was shining and all of a sudden it went dark as if someone had turned the lights out. It was dark for three hours. I peered through the darkness to make sure he was still there. There were earthquakes, things were happening all over the place and yet this guy was just having a discourse with an imaginary figure. And then there was an almighty shout. People rushed to him to see what would happen. We got a message that a great big curtain in the temple had ripped apart and there was no longer any privacy in the Jews' Holy of Holies.

At that moment this man who was half dead on the cross, spoke with a tremendous shout: 'It is finished!' and then he dismissed his spirit and seemed to be saying, 'Over to you, God.' In that moment I knew that he was who he said he was. Governor, permit me to say this. I've seen the emperors, Caesars, and we call them gods yet none of them have died such a noble death.

The testimony of the centurion, an impartial observer, was that Jesus was who he said he was.

Joseph

The next witness is Joseph of Arimathea. He had a position of authority within the Sanhedrin. He was a wealthy man. We are told in this passage that he was waiting for the kingdom of God. In another Gospel we are told that he was a 'silent witness'. That probably means that he was a believer but because of his position he was too shy to admit it. He was not prepared to be open about his faith. He believed and later he was to see.

Up to this moment he had done nothing to further the cause of Christ. But now he was more bold than any of the disciples. His moment had come. He realized that Jesus was indeed the Messiah. Isn't it interesting that he was a member of the Sanhedrin, that he had the same background as they did yet he came to an entirely different conclusion about Jesus? Look at Isaiah:

See, my servant will act wisely; he will be raised and lifted up and highly exalted. Just as there were many who were appalled at him—his appearance was so disfigured beyond that of any man and his form marred beyond human likeness, so will he sprinkle many nations, and kings will shut their mouths because of him. For what they were not told, they will see, and what they have not heard, they will understand.

Who has believed our message and to whom has the arm of the Lord been revealed? He grew up before him like a tender shoot, and like a root out of dry ground. He had no beauty or majesty to attract us to him, nothing in his appearance that we should desire him. He was despised and rejected by men, a man of sorrows, and familiar with suffering. Like one from whom men hide their faces he was despised, and we esteemed him not.

Surely he took up our infirmities and carried our sorrows, yet we considered him stricken by God, smitten by him, and afflicted. But he was pierced for our transgressions, he was crushed for our iniquities; the punishment that brought us peace was upon him, and by his wounds we are healed. We all, like sheep, have gone astray, each of us has turned to his own way; and the Lord has laid on him the iniquity of us all.

He was oppressed and afflicted, yet he did not open his mouth; he was led like a lamb to the slaughter, and as a sheep before her shearers is silent, so he did not open his mouth. By oppression and judgment he was taken away. And who can speak of his descendants? For he was cut off from the land of the living; for the transgression of my people he was stricken. He was assigned a grave with the wicked, and with the rich in his death, though he had done no violence, nor was any deceit in his mouth.

Yet it was the Lord's will to crush him and cause him to suffer, and though the Lord makes his life a guilt offering, he will see his offspring and prolong his days, and the will of the Lord will prosper in his hand. After the suffering of his soul, he will see the light of life and be satisfied; by his knowledge my righteous servant will justify many, and he will bear their iniquities. Therefore I will give him a portion among the great, and he will divide the spoils with the strong, because he poured out his life unto death, and was numbered with the transgressors. For he bore the sin of many, and made intercession for the transgressors.

Isaiah 52:13—53:12

Joseph remembered what Isaiah had written and he did backflips! He realized, 'This is my Messiah, swing open the gate! Let the king of glory come in.' Joseph had a new courage. He went and asked for the body. For Joseph it was the body of his Lord, his Saviour, the one promised of old.

Jesus fulfilled over 300 prophecies in the Old Testament. Some people tell us it just happened by coincidence, some massive coincidence. Joseph knew that no one could engineer to the letter the fulfilment of Isaiah 53 or Psalm 22. Joseph saw it and knew that his Messiah had come.

People have different attitudes towards faith in God. There are the atheists who have got their fundamental premise that God does not exist. They think that they have been everywhere, seen everything (one must suppose), know it all and they know there is no God.

Another type of person is the agnostic, like the centurion was, who said 'seeing is believing'. Believers can only show agnostics Jesus and let them make up their own minds. Perhaps, like the centurion, they will be convinced by the evidence and see that he is God.

And then there are Christians who believe that God has become a man in Jesus Christ, as witnessed to by scripture, and who have a personal relationship with him. Christ crucified is the centre of the gospel. It is the heart of our message. We have nothing to be afraid of and nothing to be ashamed of when we proclaim Christ crucified. It is the message the world needs to hear.

Conclusion

It is so easy just to read the words on the page and be left as if nothing really happened. But as we realize what Jesus actually did for us 2,000 years ago, and as we study and try to put ourselves in the shoes of the people around there, we cannot imagine the pain that he went through. We cannot know Jesus' feeling of separation from God for the first time, feeling, like a sinner, cut off from God.

Jesus could have come off the cross. He could have run away from the garden. He could have escaped, but steadfastly he set himself to fulfil the Father's plan. He was obedient to the Father in every detail. We can therefore be proud to have a king of glory who was willing to die for us, sinners that we are.

We cannot grasp how his death was sufficient to take away our sins. He died for us almost while we were slapping him in the face.

Mark 16

Alive again

When the Sabbath was over, Mary Magdalene, Mary the mother of James, and Salome bought spices so that they might go to anoint Jesus' body. Very early on the first day of the week, just after sunrise, they were on their way to the tomb and they asked each other, 'Who will roll the stone away from the entrance of the tomb?' But when they looked up, they saw that the stone, which was very large, had been rolled away.

As they entered the tomb, they saw a young man dressed in a white robe sitting on the right side, and they were alarmed. 'Don't be alarmed,' he said. 'You are looking for Jesus the Nazarene, who was crucified. He has risen! He is not here. See the place where they laid him. But go, tell his disciples and Peter, "He is going ahead of you into Galilee. There you will see him, just as he told you."'

Trembling and bewildered, the women went out and fled from the tomb. They said nothing to anyone, because they were afraid.

*[When Jesus rose early on the first day of the week, he appeared first to Mary Magdalene, out of whom he had driven seven demons. She went and told those who had been with him and who were mourning and weeping. When they heard that Jesus was alive and that she had seen him, they did not believe it. Afterwards

Jesus appeared in a different form to two of them while they were walking in the country. These returned and reported it to the rest; but they did not believe them either. Later Jesus appeared to the Eleven as they were eating; he rebuked them for their lack of faith and their stubborn refusal to believe those who had seen him after he had risen.]

* The most reliable early manuscripts and other ancient witnesses do not have Mark 16:9–20.

As well as Mark's account of the resurrection of Jesus, I want to look at the accounts in the other Gospels so that we can piece together the whole story and see exactly what happened.

The next day, the one after Preparation Day, the chief priests and the Pharisees went to Pilate. 'Sir,' they said, 'we remember that while he was still alive that deceiver said, "After three days I will rise again." So give the order for the tomb to be made secure until the third day. Otherwise, his disciples may come and steal the body and tell the people that he has been raised from the dead. This last deception will be worse than the first.'

'Take a guard,' Pilate answered. 'Go, make the tomb as secure as you know how.' So they went and made the tomb secure by putting a seal on the stone and posting the guard.

Matthew 27:62–66

After the Sabbath, at dawn on the first day of the week, Mary Magdalene and the other Mary went to look at the tomb. There was a violent earthquake, for an angel of the Lord came down from heaven and, going to the tomb, rolled back the stone and sat on it. His

*appearance was like lightning, and his clothes were
white as snow. The guards were so afraid of him that
they shook and became like dead men.*

Matthew 28:1–4

*Mary stood outside the tomb crying. As she wept,
she bent over to look into the tomb and saw two
angels in white, seated where Jesus' body had been,
one at the head and the other at the foot. They asked
her, 'Woman, why are you crying?' 'They have taken my
Lord away,' she said, 'and I don't know where they have
put him.' At this, she turned around and saw Jesus
standing there, but she did not realise that it was Jesus.
'Woman,' he said, 'why are you crying? Who is it you
are looking for?' Thinking he was the gardener, she said,
'Sir, if you have carried him away, tell me where you
have put him, and I will get him.' Jesus said to her,
'Mary.' She turned towards him and cried out in
Aramaic, 'Rabboni!' (which means Teacher).*

John 20:11–16

The chief priests and the Pharisees knew that Jesus was
dead but, because they thought Jesus had been a deceiver,
they wanted Pilate to place a unit of guards around the
tomb. The Jewish authorities were aware of the prophecy
Jesus had made that he would rise from dead and
suspected that Jesus' disciples would come and steal the
body and claim that he had risen. Pilate told them to do it
themselves, so the Jews posted a guard themselves.

The women knew that Jesus was dead. They knew he
was buried. They were coming to carry out Jewish burial
rituals. The guards too knew that Jesus was dead and
buried. To sum up the evidence to this point, there was
general agreement that Jesus was dead. The location of his
grave was public knowledge.

When the women came to the grave and saw the angel at the grave, they could not believe it. They were terrified. They were trembling. Even when Mary confronts the risen Lord, face to face—and remember she had been very close to Jesus—she does not recognize him. She did not recognize him because she did not expect to see him because he was dead and buried. When you go to put flowers on a loved one's grave, the last thing you expect is to meet the dead person!

When the disciples heard from Mary Magdalene that she had seen Jesus, their reaction was, 'Are you crazy, woman? He's dead and buried!' They did not believe it.

All the evidence confirmed that everyone knew that Jesus was dead and buried. The Jewish authorities believed that he was dead and buried. The Roman guards believed that he was dead and buried. The women believed that he was dead and buried. The disciples believed that he was dead and buried. No one was expecting the resurrection.

So if they were convinced that Jesus was dead and buried and if they were not in the remotest sense expecting the resurrection, something pretty dramatic must have happened to change their minds.

While the women were on their way, some of the guards went into the city and reported to the chief priests everything that had happened. When the chief priests had met with the elders and devised a plan, they gave the soldiers a large sum of money, telling them, 'You are to say, "His disciples came during the night and stole him away while we were asleep." If this report gets to the governor, we will satisfy him and keep you out of trouble.' So the soldiers took the money and did as they were instructed. And this story has been widely circulated among the Jews to this very day.

Matthew 28:11–15

Now when rumours of the resurrection started to spread, something had to be done to counter them. The Jews came up with an explanation. The disciples had sneaked up during the night, had evaded the guard—possibly as many as twenty soldiers—moved the stone, stolen the body, put the stone back, all while the soldiers were sleeping. Then they went around proclaiming that Jesus was risen from the dead.

This was the story that the Jews wanted to spread and it was a story which was widely believed up to the point when Matthew wrote his Gospel.

There are two vitally important questions to be answered now: Who moved the stone? Where is the body? There are immediately three prime suspects.

Suspect 1: The Roman guards

Sentry duty was their job. For a guard to be found asleep on duty was punishable by death. So that is why the Jews had to assure the soldiers that if they stuck to their story they would protect them. Otherwise the entire guard would have been executed for gross neglect of duty. But what motive would the guards have had? Why would they have wanted to perpetuate a myth that Jesus had risen from the dead? The Romans were keen to preserve the Pax Romana, the peace in the empire. So it would not make sense for them to risk encouraging a riot by putting a deception about.

Suspect 2: The Jewish authorities

Do we really think the Jewish authorities would go down and move the stone? If the Jews had known where the body of Jesus was, years later when Christianity was spreading and the Christians were bumping their gums, do you not think they would have just have produced the decaying body and said 'Here is your God?'

I think we can dismiss the Romans and the Jews as serious suspects in the conspiracy.

Suspect 3: The disciples

Did the disciples steal the body? In the ancient world women had no place in the authority structure. Anyone wanting to set out and disseminate a great new theory or philosophy would never think of having women as the first and crucial witnesses to their theory.

Wrong tomb?

Maybe the women made a mistake. Maybe they went to the wrong tomb, not knowing where Jesus was buried. But we are told that 'Mary Magdalene and Mary the mother of Joseph saw where he was laid' (Mark 15:47).

The women followed Joseph and saw where the grave was. The women saw the soldiers. So the grave they came to was the one they had seen Jesus buried in and it was a tomb guarded by soldiers. I can't imagine there were many tombs with armed guards around them in that part of Jerusalem that day.

Also Mary loved Jesus intimately and the other Mary was his mother. How many mothers would forget where their son was buried? Would it not be indelibly etched on their minds for life?

All in the mind?

Were the women hallucinating, because they were so pumped up? Look at John 20:15, when Mary has an encounter in the garden: 'Woman,' he said, 'why are you crying? Who is it you are looking for?' Thinking he was the gardener, she said, 'Sir, if you have carried him away, tell me where you have put him, and I will get him.'

When people hallucinate, they see things and believe they are something that they are not. If Mary had been hallucinating, she would have seen the gardener and thought he was the Christ. Yet in reality, Mary saw Jesus and thought he was the gardener. The facts are that Mary was not expecting to see Jesus and when she did see him she didn't recognize that it was Jesus.

Jesus had a way of speaking to Mary that made Mary recognize him immediately. But even then she ran off in fear and trembling. It was no hallucination. Mary saw what she never expected to see.

Remember too Jesus' appearance to the two disciples on the road to Emmaus. They did not recognize him either. Jesus walked with them for hours and still they did not recognize him. If they were looking for Jesus and hallucinating, wouldn't they have seen him in everyone they met on the road rather than not recognizing him when he was walking with them?

Another problem with the hallucination theory is the 500 people who saw him at one time, referred to in Corinthians. Paul was able to say that many of them were still alive when he was writing. Did they all have the same hallucination? I think not.

In Mark 16:9 we read: 'When Jesus rose early on the first day of the week, he appeared first to Mary Magdalene, out of whom he had driven seven demons.' In other words, she was bonkers, off her tree. It was Jesus who healed her and restored her self-esteem. Mary did not need a Messiah. Jesus had done enough for her. What was it that changed her?

The apostles

Let us look at the apostles, those great big towering strengths of Christianity, or do I mean those weak, scared, frightened, shaken men who had followed Jesus for two and a half years? They had given up their jobs as fishermen or tax-collectors to follow the Messiah. Then in the garden of Gethsemane they all fled. Are we expected to believe that this shaken scared bunch of guys stole the body and hid it and then sent this myth down the annals of history? No, the disciples were not expecting this kind of Messiah. Remember Peter in his greatest moment in Mark 8. Jesus had asked: 'Who do people say I am?' and Peter had given him the right answer. The passage continues: 'He then began to teach them that the Son of Man must suffer many things and be rejected by the elders, chief priests and teachers of the law, and that he must be killed and after three days rise again. He spoke plainly about this, and Peter took him aside and began to rebuke him' (Mark 8:31–32).

The highlight of Peter's ministry in the Gospels: yet the very next moment when Jesus told Peter about his suffering, Peter rebuked Jesus and said: 'You cannot be my Messiah and yet talk about suffering.' Peter was looking for a Messiah who was a knight in shining armour. Peter went on to deny the Lord three times, he was so scared. All of a sudden his dreams were shattered.

James went on to be the leader of the church in Jerusalem. Yet in the Gospels we read that James and the rest of Jesus' brothers and sisters thought he was mad the way he went around preaching. James didn't believe he was the Messiah. What changed his mind?

What about John? Remember James and John, the sons of thunder, and how they wanted to sit one on the right and one on the left in heaven. If he had lived in our day, John could have been the one who shot Prime Minister Rabin. He was a zealot. What was it that changed them? Was it stealing a body and peddling a deception? Was that what changed their lives?

There have been many examples throughout history of people dying for what they believe in. But would people die for what they know to be a lie? Peter, who had been a complete coward and denied that he knew Jesus, died for his faith in the resurrection. James likewise was faithful to death in his belief in the resurrection.

Look at 1 Corinthians 15:12–19:

*B*ut *if it is preached that Christ has been raised from the dead, how can some of you say that there is no resurrection of the dead? If there is no resurrection of the dead, then not even Christ has been raised. And if Christ has not been raised, our preaching is useless and so is your faith. More than that, we are then found to be false witnesses about God, for we have testified about God that he raised Christ from the dead. But he did not raise him if in fact the dead are not raised. For if the dead are not raised, then Christ has not been raised either. And if Christ has not been raised, your faith is futile; you are still in your sins. Then those also who have fallen asleep in Christ are lost. If only for this life we have hope in Christ, we are to be pitied more than all men.*

Paul stresses the importance of the resurrection to what we believe. If the resurrection is disproved, everything goes out the window.

Peter, too, stresses the importance of the resurrection: 'We did not follow cleverly invented stories when we told you about the power and coming of our Lord Jesus Christ, but we were eye-witnesses of his majesty' (2 Peter 1:16).

Thomas the apostle
When Thomas was told that Jesus had risen, he was sceptical.

*S*o *the other disciples told him, 'We have seen the Lord!' But he said to them, 'Unless I see the nail*

*marks in his hands and put my finger where the nails
were, and put my hand into his side, I will not believe it.'
A week later his disciples were in the house again,
and Thomas was with them. Though the doors were
locked, Jesus came and stood among them and said,
'Peace be with you!' Then he said to Thomas, 'Put your
finger here; see my hands. Reach out your hand and put
it into my side. Stop doubting and believe.' Thomas said
to him, 'My Lord and my God!'*

John 20:25–28

Guess what happened? Jesus came in, again walking
through the wall. Imagine how Thomas reacted. 'I don't
believe it. Let me check you out. Things like that don't
happen. My Lord and my God!' Thomas was a real sceptic.
What changed him? At the end of the day arguably the
greatest evidence for the fact of the resurrection is changed
lives.

Peter saw the risen Christ. John saw him. James saw
him. Mary saw him. The 500 saw him. Their lives were
changed so much that people saw that something must
have happened to change them.

The question is: Can people tell from the things that we
do that we are Christians? Has our encounter with Jesus
changed our lives? People could tell that the early Church
were Christians by how they lived. Can people tell that we
are Christians or do we live as Christians on Sunday and
worship pleasure or materialism the rest of the week? How
do you define yourself: mother, father, banker, sportsman?
Paul said: 'For to me, to live is Christ and to die is gain'
(Philippians 1:21), a tough challenge for each and every
one of us.

Any literature on Christians in classical antiquity will
show you how people died frequently for their belief in the
resurrection, but it was the change in their lives as a result

of their encounter with the risen Lord that won them converts and enemies. Has your life been changed like that?

If you have enjoyed reading *On Your Mark*, you may wish to know that The Bible Reading Fellowship publishes a regular series of Bible reading notes, *New Daylight*, which is published three times a year (in January, May and September) and contains printed Bible passages, brief comments and prayers. *New Daylight* is also available in a large print version.

Copies of *New Daylight* may be obtained from your local Christian bookshop or by subscription direct from BRF.

A free sample copy of *New Daylight* containing two weeks of readings may be obtained by sending an A5 SAE marked '*New Daylight*' to BRF.

For more information about *New Daylight* and the full range of BRF publications, write to: The Bible Reading Fellowship, Peter's Way, Sandy Lane West, Oxford OX4 5HG (Tel. 01865 748227)

ALSO BY KRISS AKABUSI

In *Kriss Akabusi On Track with the Bible*, Kriss shares his own enthusiasm for the Bible and talks about passages which are particularly special to him.

'Kriss' message is… work hard, achieve all you can, but ultimately without God you won't find meaning and satisfaction in life.' **Stuart Weir, Director, Christians in Sport**

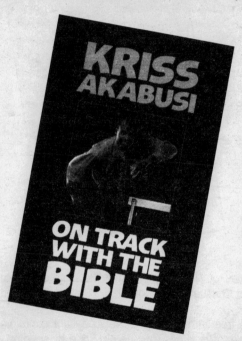

Kriss Akabusi On Track with the Bible may be obtained from your local Christian bookshop or, in case of difficulty, direct from The Bible Reading Fellowship, Peter's Way, Sandy Lane West, Oxford OX4 5HG (Tel. 01865 748227)